An Early Resurrection is two things: the candid report of an ardent soul on its quest for redemption, and the reflections of a philosopher on the gospel and time. It will appeal to readers who manage their religious struggles by thinking, as Adam Miller does so productively.

—Richard Lyman Bushman
author of Joseph Smith: Rough Stone Rolling

You will look at the world differently after reading this book. *An Early Resurrection* will help you see many things in a new light: the Book of Mormon, Paul's New Testament writings, gospel ordinances, people you meet, your stress over too many deadlines, and time itself (*especially* time itself). Miller's book offers a deeper understanding of what it means to be alive in Christ *now*, in the *present*. And you'll care for, and care about, the present in a way that can only come with being alive.

—J.B. Haws
*Assistant Professor of Church History and Doctrine
Brigham Young University*

This is a book about time—particularly Christ's ability to defy, fold, and reorder time for our benefit. In a wonderfully fresh, thought-provoking approach, Adam Miller effectively challenges readers to live today as though Christ's promises were already realities. Because they are. An ideal read for anyone seeking the authentic life—a life in Christ.

—Camille Fronk Olson
*Professor of Ancient Scripture
Brigham Young University*

An Early Resurrection

Life in Christ
before You Die

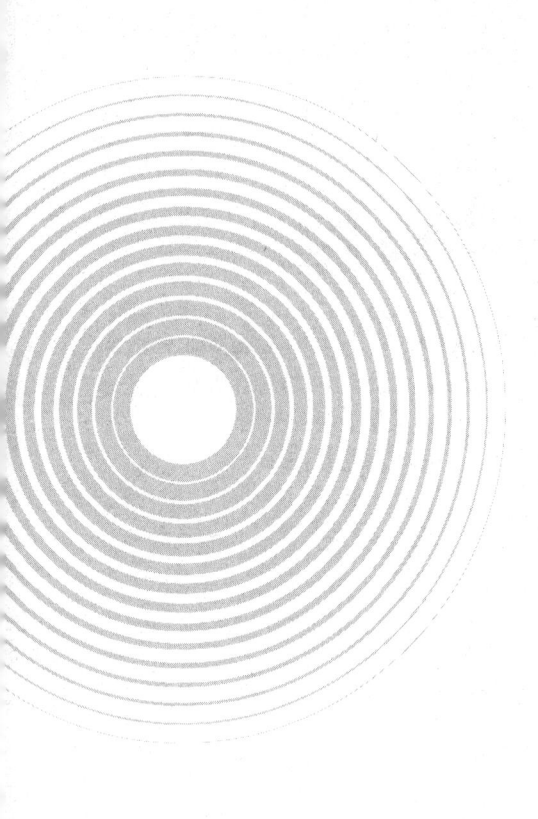

An Early Resurrection

Life in Christ
before You Die

Adam S. Miller

For Stan Hall

Library of Congress Cataloging-in-Publication Data

Names: Miller, Adam S., author.
Title: An early resurrection : life in Christ before you die / Adam S. Miller.
Description: Salt Lake City, Utah : Deseret Book, [2018] | Includes bibliographical references.
Identifiers: LCCN 2017059813 | ISBN 9781629723686 (paperbound)
Subjects: LCSH: Christian life—Mormon authors. | The Church of Jesus Christ of Latter-day Saints—Doctrines. | Mormon Church—Doctrines.
Classification: LCC BX8656 .M524 2018 | DDC 248.4/89332—dc23
LC record available at https://lccn.loc.gov/2017059813

Printed in the United States of America
LSC Communications, Crawfordsville, IN

10   9   8   7   6   5   4

Think of yourself as dead.
You have lived your life.
Now take what's left
and live it properly.

—MARCUS AURELIUS

Contents

Contents

Preface

This isn't an ordinary church book. My day job as a philosophy professor is to blame.

Every day I get up and go to work and spend my time thinking about the kinds of things that most people take for granted. While it's normal to ask if some particular thing is real or true or good, my job is to ask what it *means* for something to be real or true or good in the first place. While it's normal to ask if some particular thing exists, my job is to ask instead about what it means to exist at all. And while it's normal to ask what time of day it is, my job is to ask about time itself. As a philosopher, I ask, What *is* time, anyway?

These are hard questions. They're slippery and

abstract. They gum up our routines. They're not very practical.

But, still, living with these questions has changed me in practical ways. Working with them every day, they've bled back into my everyday life. They've come to color even my ordinary decisions as they show me new ways to think about my life and my religion.

This book, *An Early Resurrection*, is one example of how my work in philosophy has come to color my everyday life. For years now I've been focused on scholarly projects that ask about the nature of time, and this work has, especially, changed how I think about Christ. The more I've thought about time, the more I've come to think about Christ's atonement in terms of time. I've come to think about the atonement in terms of how Christ solves the problem of time, in terms of how he redeems time, and in terms of how he reorders my experience of time.

When Nicodemus comes to Jesus at night,

I've come to think about the atonement in terms of how Christ solves the problem of time, in terms of how he redeems time, and in terms of how he reorders my experience of time.

Christ tells him that "except a man be born again, he cannot see the kingdom of God" (John 3:3). Nicodemus isn't sure what this means. He can't see how a grown man could, in the middle of life, go back to the beginning and start over. "How can a man be born when he is old? can he enter the second time into his mother's womb, and be born?" (John 3:4). This is, I think, a serious question. Nicodemus is asking a question about time.

In our ordinary experience of time, beginnings only come at the beginning and ends only come at the end. But Christ is promising something else. The beginning, he promises, can come again. The beginning can come in the middle. Even in the middle of life, we can be born again and begin a new life. "Marvel not that I said unto thee, Ye must be born again. The wind bloweth where it listeth, and thou hearest the sound thereof, but canst not tell whence it cometh, and whither it goeth: so is every one that is born of the Spirit" (John 3:7–8). Those who are born of the Spirit are mysterious to outsiders in exactly this way. Their lives don't follow time's normal rules. Things happen out of order for them. They're like the wind. When they pass your way, you can feel that something is happening with them, but you can't tell where they started or where they're going.

The apostle Paul plays with this same idea. However, instead of talking about Christ's work of redeeming time in terms of a late (or second) birth, he describes it as a kind of *early resurrection* that gets underway even before we die (cf. Galatians 2:19–20). In either case, though, the basic idea is the same. When I start a new life in Christ, Christ reorders my experience of time. The beginning comes in the middle, the end comes before the beginning, and the ordinary stuff of life is saved as we live it.

This whole book is a meditation on just this one idea: the idea that starting a new life in Christ can be described as an early resurrection and that this kind of early resurrection is intended to save both my future *and* my present. Following this thread, I'll look at how Paul defines a "life in Christ," how ordinances function as types of Christ, how Christ uses types to reorder our experience of time and fulfill God's law, how people in the Book of Mormon managed to live as though Christ had already come long before he was born, how sacred covenants fold the future into the present, and how the temple itself bends time in order to seal generations of parents and children into a single family.

I will, of course, tend toward the philosophical as I work my way through these ideas—for better or worse, this is the gift I have to give. But I hope that, in addition to finding this a little unusual, you will also find it useful.

This whole book is a meditation on just this one idea: the idea that starting a new life in Christ can be described as an early resurrection and that this kind of early resurrection is intended to save both my future *and* my present.

Though this book frequently mentions God, it is primarily centered on Christ and what it means to find a new "life in Christ." This emphasis results primarily from the weight I give to the kind of language used in both Paul's epistles and the Book of Mormon. But I take it for granted that, as Christ explains to Philip, "he that hath seen [Christ] hath seen the Father" (John 14:9).

Also, I want to acknowledge up front that there is nothing definitive or authoritative about the work I do in this book. I haven't received any special revelations. I'm just an ordinary Mormon who has read a lot of books. All I can offer here is just one way among many to talk about Christ, and, like any way of talking, this way has its strengths and weaknesses. Though I'm happy to acknowledge the help and support of my wife, my family, Blair Hodges, Jenny Webb, Rosalynde Welch, and Kylie Turley, among others, I alone am responsible for this book's weaknesses. Take what is helpful and leave the rest.

1

As Though He Had Already Come

The Book of Mormon unlocks a biblical understanding of Christ.

The Book of Mormon is a key. The Bible is a door. It's not enough for me to shelve them side by side. It's not enough to read the one and then the other. I need to slot the key, turn the tumblers, and open the door.

The Bible needs a key because "many plain and precious things" were "taken away" (1 Nephi 13:28). The Book of Mormon is meant to return what was lost and "make known" these "plain and precious things" by declaring that "the Lamb of God is the Son of the Eternal Father, and the Savior of the world; and that all men must come unto him, or they cannot be saved" (v. 40). The

1

Book of Mormon unlocks the Bible by making Christ plain.

The Book of Mormon clarifies many biblical ideas, but, in the end, it basically rings the same Christian bells. As Nephi says, "we talk of Christ, we rejoice in Christ, we preach of Christ, we prophesy of Christ, and we write according to our prophecies" (2 Nephi 25:26). Clearly, the Book of Mormon is meant to be a second witness of Christ. The big difference between the Bible and the Book of Mormon is not *what* is said but *when* it is said. Nephi and company are rejoicing—and living—in Christ long before Christ comes. This anachrony is no accident. Book of Mormon prophets are extraordinarily self-conscious about their peculiar, anticipatory brand of pre-Christian Christianity. In a crucial verse (to which I will return), Jarom claims, four hundred years before Christ, that their prophets worked day and night to persuade the people to do just one thing: "to look forward unto the Messiah, and believe in him to come *as though he already was*" (Jarom 1:11, emphasis added). This is what's different about Nephite Christianity: they lived in Christ before Christ came. They lived Christ's future in their present.

This, it seems to me, is a truth that's muted in

our Bible. And, more, it's the kind of truth that matters not because it settles a debate but because it frames how to live as a Christian. It's precious because it shows something vital about the shape of a Christian life, regardless of when that life happens to be lived. This is what the Book of Mormon makes plain: to live a Christian life is to live in Christ *as if he were already present*. As a Christian, I, like the Nephites, must learn to live as though Christ were already here. I must learn to live time out of order. For the Nephites, the temptation

> This is what the Book of Mormon makes plain: to live a Christian life is to live in Christ *as if he were already present.*

was to think that Christ only belonged to the future. For me, the temptation is to think that Christ only belongs to the past (or, again, to some future world). Either way, the temptation is to think that Christ does not belong to the present. But a past or future Christ is not enough. It is not enough for me to believe in the past or future *idea* of Christ. To be Christian, I have to learn how to share my *life* with Christ in the present.

Trying to explain to his struggling congregations what a Christian life looks like, Paul has to address the same basic problem as the Nephites. In his letters, he has to ask, What does it mean to live in Christ when Christ has not yet come? Though, for Paul, this question takes a slightly different form. Paul has to ask, What does it mean to live in Christ when Christ, already risen, has not yet come *again*? The answer, though, is the same. Whether I'm waiting for Christ's first coming or his second, my job is to live in Christ as though he were already here. My job is to live, right now, as if I had already passed through death's veil and into the presence of God. My job is to live my promised redemption in the present tense.

Paul's powerful explanation of how faith and law fit together to define a Christian life unfolds in line with this question, as an answer to this problem. In particular, it unfolds in line with a prophetic logic—a logic plainly on display in the Book of Mormon—that interleaves the future with the present in order to save my life both now and later.

This is good news. It's news I need to hear. It's doubtless true that I've lived an ordinary life with only ordinary failings—even as a sinner, I'm unexceptional. But it has still been hard for me to believe that Christ could, in the end, save me. It took a long time for me to believe that some kind of future with Christ was possible. If there's a minimum bar for finding forgiveness and qualifying for sainthood, I didn't see how I could meet it. For this hope in Christ to grow, I needed time. I needed to let some ideas and ambitions go. I had to learn about obedience and service and discipline. I had to learn some humility. I had to learn something about how to pray. But, as I worked at this, something else happened. Christ, like a thief in the night, came when I wasn't looking (cf. 1 Thessalonians 5:2). Before I was ready, he broke into the present and claimed me as his own. Christ, the life of the world, showed up, unannounced, in the daily living of my ordinary life. I discovered Christ in the same way an old fish finally discovers water: not in a supernatural vision but in a revelation of the bare, God-given fact that I could see anything at all.

> Christ, the life of the world, showed up, unannounced, in the daily living of my ordinary life.

This isn't what I expected. I expected to struggle my whole life to earn a distant future with Christ. I expected to patiently curate my life for decades as some kind of winning proof that—possibly, eventually—I might deserve to live in God's presence. Instead, I found

Christ impatient to save me. I found Christ already wanting to share my mortal life. I found Christ wanting to live *in* me. I'd been living as if the day of miracles had not yet come, as if revelations had ceased, as if God were dead or asleep, as if Christ were fine china locked away for a special occasion at the end of time (cf. Moroni 7:35–38). But this wasn't the case.

Surprised by Christ, I've had to learn something new. I've had to learn what the Book of Mormon was trying to show. I've had to learn how to live, right now, as though Christ had already come. I've had to learn how to believe not just in continuing revelation but in continuing redemption. I've had to learn to believe in an early resurrection.

2

An Early Resurrection

Redemption and even resurrection aren't just for the next world. They can also be part of this life and these bodies, here and now.

In Christ, it's possible to die while you're still alive. And having died early, it's possible for your resurrection to begin before you've even left this world.

In Christ, time's grip loosens and things start happening out of order. This is what a Christian life looks like: you're born, you're buried with Christ, your resurrection begins, and *then* you die. If Christ has his way, we'll all die before we're dead and every one of us will yield our lives, here and now, to an early resurrection.

If I keep this promise at arm's length, it's because I'm afraid. I don't want to die. I don't want to give

> In Christ, time's grip loosens and things start happening out of order.

up my life. But this, as Paul describes it, is how redemption works. "I am crucified with Christ: nevertheless I live; yet not I, but Christ liveth in me: and the life which I now live in the flesh I live by the faith of the Son of God, who loved me, and gave himself for me" (Galatians 2:20). Though my "old man is crucified with him," still, I live (Romans 6:6). And this new life is lived not just in the spirit but "in the flesh." This redeemed body is real, but it's no longer simply mine. It's Christ's. And if I already share in his resurrection, it's because he now lives in me. Dying to my old life, I've surrendered my name and life for his.

This is what I promised when I was baptized. This is what I promised in the temple. This is what I promise again each week with the sacrament. I promise to turn my life over to God, to consecrate the whole of it, and I promise to do so now, not later. I promise to let go of my own name and "take his name upon me" (cf. D&C 20:77). I promise to always remember him. I promise to think what he would think, to say what he would say, to do what he would do. I promise to pray for his will to be done, not mine. I promise to be part of the body of Christ. I promise to let the light and life of *his* resurrection shine in me.

In this sense, resurrection isn't only for the next life. It's meant, all the more, for my troubled present. If I insist on postponing my death, then I also insist on postponing my redemption. But if I'm willing to let those selfish parts of me die now—long before my body fails and my heart stops—then Christ's resurrection can also begin to take hold of my body now. I can share in Christ's life in this world and in this flesh.

This is the promise: "As Christ was raised up from the dead by the glory of the Father, even so we also should walk in newness of life. For if we have been planted together in the likeness of his death, we shall be also in the likeness of his resurrection" (Romans 6:4–5).

3

Life in Christ

"Life in Christ" is a name for what
redemption and resurrection look like—
and feel like—in this mortal world.

Eternal life is the promise that death is not the end,
that there is life after death. It's the promise that
both my body and this world can continue after
death in the presence of God. And this promise
matters. As Paul says, "If in this life only we have
hope in Christ, we are of all men most miserable"
(1 Corinthians 15:19). But the reverse is also true.
If for the *next* life only I have hope in Christ, I am
also lost. By itself, even the glory of an eternal life
is not enough.

Without losing sight of eternal life, Paul calls
this nearer mortal hope "life in Christ." For Paul,
to be a Christian in this world is to be *in* Christ. As
a Christian I must hope in Christ (1 Corinthians

15:19), rejoice in Christ (Philippians 3:3), have faith in Christ (Galatians 3:26), be wise in Christ (1 Corinthians 4:10), speak the truth in Christ (Romans 9:1), pray in Christ (2 Corinthians 5:20), be created in Christ (Ephesians 2:10), love in Christ (2 Timothy 1:13), triumph in Christ (2 Corinthians 2:14), sleep in Christ (1 Corinthians 15:18), trust in Christ (Ephesians 1:12), be one in Christ (Galatians 3:28), find consolation in Christ (Philippians 2:1), and, of course, live in Christ (Romans 8:2). Everything I do, I must do it in Christ.

This "in" is decisive. It's the difference between life and death. It's the difference between wanting love and being in love. Something changes when you are in love. It's not just that a new person is added to your life, one person among many. It's that this new person changes for you what it means to be alive. Life is no longer just lived. Now, life is lived *in* love. You may keep the same job, have the same friends, and eat the same food, but something basic about why you do these things, or even *how* you do them, will have changed. This difference may be obvious or subtle, but it will certainly be

> Like being in love, living in Christ changes what it means to be alive.

deep. In love, life as a whole feels different. You see what you didn't used to see. You hear what you didn't used to hear. You care for things you'd ignored. You become capable of doing things that, last week, you weren't able to do.

Life in Christ is like this. In Christ, the way I live—my manner of living—is changed from the inside out. Like being in love, living in Christ changes what it means to be alive. Living in Christ, I carry myself differently. I desire differently. I love differently. I greet pain and loss differently. I fail differently. I succeed differently. I part with the past differently. I respond to the present differently. I look to the future differently. In Christ, I hold time itself in a very different way.

> Rather than just storing up salvation for the future, life in Christ saves my life *as I'm living it.*

In the end, this last difference is the biggest. Life is made out of time. To live a different kind of life in Christ is to live time itself in a different way. Living in Christ, I discover a new way of being in time. In Christ, I repent. The past no longer owns me, the present isn't held at arm's length, and the future stops undermining me. Instead of waiting for Christ, I find that Christ is already given. I wake up to discover what was true all along, that

Christ is "not far from every of one of us: for in him we live, and move, and have our being" (Acts 17:27–28).

This, at root, is what life in Christ looks like. Life in Christ turns on a new way of handling time. Rather than just storing up salvation for the future, life in Christ saves my life *as I'm living it.* In Christ, the veil grows thin and eternity starts bleeding into time. The next life, a life lived in the presence of God, gets underway before I've even died.

4

The Feel of a
Life in Christ

Life in Christ isn't just a doctrine
or idea. It's real, material, and
palpable. It has a certain "feel."

What does the onset of an early resurrection *feel* like? What does it feel like to live in Christ, here and now? What does it feel like to hold time in a new way? What does it feel like to find eternity already pushing into the present?

Life in Christ has a certain feel. It's not just an idea. It doesn't just change how I think. Life in Christ goes deeper than this. It's in my body, my heart, my lungs, my muscles and blood and bones. It glows like a burning coal in my belly. Life in Christ feels like being alive. It feels—in all its ordinary sensitivity, difficulty, and complexity—like what being alive feels like.

What, then, makes life in Christ different from

just being alive? Almost nothing. The difference is that, alive in Christ, I stop looking beyond my life for something other than life. I stop looking past my life for something special or mysterious. I stop being blind to the life I'm already living. What Jacob says about scripture is even more true about life: "Wherefore, because of their blindness, which blindness came by looking beyond the mark, they must needs fall; for God hath taken away his plainness from them, and delivered unto them many things which they cannot understand, because they desired it" (Jacob 4:14). In Christ, I stop desiring what I can't understand, I *stop* looking beyond the mark, and, as a result, what is plain and precious (my "plain old life") is no longer hidden from me.

> The difference between being alive and being alive in Christ is like the difference between seeing *things* in the light and seeing the *light* that lets me see things.

The difference between being alive and being alive in Christ is like the difference between seeing *things* in the light and seeing the *light* that lets me see things. In either case, both the things and the light are the same. But, in the second case, things couldn't look more different. God is trying to give me the light itself—so plain, so obvious, so ordinary—but I'm running around at noonday looking for some special *thing* in the light, blind to the light. Christ, as the light of the world, is hidden in plain sight.

It's true that, even when I am blind to Christ, I am already alive and feeling. But, alive in Christ, I finally start to *feel* what feeling alive feels like. When this happens, I stop trying to *think* that Christ is real and I *feel* that he is. A testimony takes root when I feel Christ in my flesh. It takes root when I feel Christ in the same way I feel, without thinking, which direction is up or whether ice is cold. It happens when I feel Christ immediately, viscerally, a notch or two deeper than my mind.

As a practical matter, much of life in Christ boils down to learning this one thing: how to feel, rather than flee, these feelings. All the basic things we do in the church—prayer, scripture study, sacrament meeting, visiting teaching, temple attendance—are meant to cultivate this sensitivity. Living in Christ, I become sensitive to the feel of life, to the feel of the Spirit, as it passes through my body. This feeling is both familiar and strange. It is both ordinary and divine. As Parley Pratt describes it, Spirit has just this effect. It resurrects my flesh, clears my mind, and opens my senses:

> The gift of the Holy Spirit adapts it-self to all these organs or attributes. It quickens all the intellectual faculties, in-creases, enlarges, expands and purifies all the natural passions and affections; and adapts them, by the gift of wisdom, to their lawful use. It inspires, develops, cultivates and matures all the fine toned sympathies, joys, tastes, kindred feelings and affections of our nature. It inspires virtue, kindness, goodness, tenderness, gentleness and charity. It develops beauty of person, form and features. It tends to health, vigour, animation and social feel-ing. It develops and invigorates all the faculties of the physical and intellectual man. It strengthens, invigorates, and gives tone to the nerves. In short, it is, as it were, marrow to the bone, joy to the heart, light to the eyes, music to the ears, and life to the whole being.[1]

---

1. Parley P. Pratt, *Key to the Science of Theology* (Liverpool: F. D. Richards, 1855), 98–99.

Driving for days, I can forget that I'm driving. I can get lost in my head for hours on end, locked in loops of worry and fantasy, until something jars me back into the present and back into the driver's seat. Who was driving the car all that time? Who changed lanes? Who braked? How much of my life have I lived like this, pale and inattentive? How long have I gone without Spirit, dazed and desensitized? Hours? Days? Weeks? Have I mishandled time for years on end? How much of my life has, without Christ, slipped by *unlived*? How rarely do I manage to see the light?

> In Christ, I return to the present and discover, in being present, the presence of God.

Open to life and sensitized by Spirit, I stop daydreaming and remember that I'm already alive. I remember to *feel* that I'm alive. In Christ, I return to the present and discover, in being present, the presence of God. Filled with the Spirit, I get a local dose of Christ's resurrection.

5

Ordinances Show Us How to Live in Christ

Ordinances are doors that open onto life in Christ. They not only prepare us for the next world but teach us how to handle time differently in this one.

It's possible, of course, to be alive and to forget what being alive feels like. It's possible to live in a way that avoids life. And, thus, it's possible to live in a way that avoids Christ, the giver of that life. Life in Christ depends on a certain way of being alive, on a certain manner of living. And this way of life turns on my willingness to feel what I'm feeling. And, more than this, it turns on my willingness to care for the whole of what feeling alive entails.

Our rituals and ordinances are important because they teach us how to care. They distill this manner of Christlike living into symbols. They condense this way of handling time into repeatable gestures. Our rituals display the shape of a life grounded in Christ. As section 84 claims, "In the ordinances thereof, the power of godliness is manifest" and "without this no man can see the face of God, even the Father, and live" (D&C 84:20, 22). Our rituals are powerful because they display, in outline, the profile of this godly life. And, living in this godly way, I'm empowered to enter God's presence. I'm empowered to live.

> Our rituals display the shape of a life grounded in Christ.

Alma makes a similar point about ordinances. He explains that "the Lord God ordained priests, after his holy order," and that "those priests were ordained after the order of his Son, in a manner that thereby the people might know in what manner to look forward to his Son for redemption" (Alma 13:1–2). For Alma, these priests are important because their ordination displays—for men and women alike—something crucial about the shape of a life in Christ. Life in Christ unfolds according to an ordained pattern, in line with a certain order. It lines up with what Alma calls "the order of the Son." And this order is powerful because it can *reorder* my experience of time in a way that redeems it.

How does this work? How can an ordinance reorder time and reconnect me with what it feels like to be alive? According to Alma, there is something about the "manner" of this ritual that can show us how to look forward to Christ for redemption. This manner is the key. It's this certain manner of looking forward that, in Christ, reorders my experience of time and kickstarts an early resurrection. God's power is manifest in these ordinances because they reveal this new way of looking forward, this new way of handling time.

Say, it's an ordinary Sunday. I'm sitting in a pew with my family. I see the bread broken. I hear the prayers said. I see the emblems passed from hand to hand, Christ's body and blood shared among us. And in that moment, if I'm paying attention, time can unfold differently. The normal pull of time, of the inevitable chain of cause and effect, can be broken. I can be forgiven. The grip of my past can loosen. My fears for the future can

> God's power is manifest in these ordinances because they reveal this new way of looking forward, this new way of handling time.

lessen. I can be present. And, in the present, I can be empowered to "look forward" in a new way. Rather than simply looking through the present and into the future—to church being over, to the game on Tuesday, to summer vacation—I can learn to see in the present what is already given and what is already needed.

6

The Rest of the Lord

Living in Christ, I'm empowered to enter
"the rest of the Lord." This rest, rather
than being an escape from time, arrives
as a new way of handling time.

What does this new way of handling time look
like? Alma offers some additional explanation. He
says: "Now these ordinances were given after this
manner, that thereby the people might look forward on the Son of God, it being a type of his order, or it being his order, and this that they might
look forward to him for a remission of their sins,
that they might enter into the rest of the Lord"
(Alma 13:16).

These ordinances were given in a certain manner, a manner intended to show each of us how to
enter into what Alma calls "the rest of the Lord."
This kind of rest is a very precise description of
what the onset of a resurrected life in Christ feels

like. In my everyday life, fallen and forgetful, I feel the weight of time. Time is heavy and demanding. I rush from place to place. I forget where I am and what matters. I feel guilty about the past. I'm bored by the present. I'm stressed about the future. There's never enough time. It's hard to sleep at night. Anger and regret are close at hand. Life is slipping away.

> But Christ is offering something else. Not just rest in the next life, but rest *as a way of life*.

But Christ is offering something else. Not just rest in the next life, but rest *as a way of life*. Life in Christ offers a way of handling time that allows us to enter into the rest of the Lord right now. Living in Christ, we live and move and have our being *in* this state of rest. The effect of this rest is immediate and bodily. In Christ, the pounding in my head goes quiet. The knots in my neck loosen. My teeth stop grinding and my fists unclench. And, even while I'm busy at work, I can feel, deep in my gut, a poised, powerful, radiating silence.

Entering into this rest depends, as Alma puts it, on learning "in what manner to look forward to the Son of God" (Alma 13:2). That is, this new life in Christ depends on learning a new way of "looking forward." If I spend my life looking forward to the wrong things—or, even more to the point, if I spend my life looking forward in the wrong *way*—then I'll miss this rest. In fact, I'll miss out on life itself. I'll spend my life wishing I was someplace else, with someone else, enjoying something else, and miss what's right in front of me. Dreaming about a future life, I'll forget what it feels like to be alive. Avoiding life in the present, I'll avoid Christ. I'll be lost. I'll feel numb. I'll be angry. I'll feel dead.

One more detail is crucial here. In addition to the rest of the Lord, Alma claims that these ordinances matter because, in relation to Christ, they "are a type of his order" and, as types, they show us how "to look forward to him for a remission of our sins" (Alma 13:16). These types show us *how* to enter into the rest of the Lord. They show us this new way of looking forward. These ordinances have something to say about the manner in which we should look forward to Christ because, as ordinances, they are themselves "a type and a shadow of things which are to come" (Mosiah

> Dreaming about a future life, I'll forget what it feels like to be alive. Avoiding life in the present, I'll avoid Christ.

13:10). As a shadow of what is to come, a type is a symbol that allows what has not yet happened to—nonetheless—appear as already present.

This is the key. Types are important because they reveal the shape of a life in Christ. Types allow our future resurrection in Christ to show up early, in this world, in this life, in this mortal body.

7

Types of Christ

Types are symbols that reorder time.
They make what is promised present.

Types are symbols. Like all symbols, they stand in for something else. They work, like Christ, vicariously. Instead of handing you a rock, I can use a symbol, like a drawing, to stand in for that rock. Instead of taking you by the arm, I can call your name. Types work this same way. By standing in for something else, they can take what is distant and make it present.

But types are a specific kind of symbol. Rather than standing in for something that exists in some other *place*, types stand in for things that exist in some other

Types open a door to a new way of handling time. They allow the future to take hold in the present.

time. Types, like prophecies, connect us with the future. But, unlike prophecies, types don't just predict the future. Rather, they *stand in* for that future, right now, making it present. In this way, types open a door to a new way of handling time. They allow the future to take hold in the present.

Types are important for Paul. In Greek, the word Paul uses is *typos*. In the KJV, it's often rendered as "figure." In Romans 5:14, for instance, Paul describes Adam as a type or figure of Christ. Adam, he says, "is the figure of him that was to come." Paul sees Adam's role as prefiguring the redemptive part eventually played by Christ. As Adam is the first man in the old world, Christ is the first man in the new world. Right from the start, in Adam's own person, the end was visibly stamped into the beginning. Right from the start, Christ's future was crowding into and redeeming our very human past.

> Like a type, life in Christ superimposes my future resurrection onto my present experience. It stamps Christ's immortal seal directly into the wax of my mortal life.

The Greek word for "type" literally means the stroke of a blow or the mark left by that blow. This is a useful image.

As with a typewriter or a manual printing press, a type is the imprint left by a blow. Like a type, life in Christ superimposes my future resurrection onto my present experience. It stamps Christ's immortal seal directly into the wax of my mortal life. With a measured blow, without waiting for time to end, it imprints eternity onto time.

This is the difficulty of living in Christ. I have to do two things at once: (1) rather than just succumbing to the pull of time, I have to hang on to eternity, and (2) rather than just escaping into what's timeless, I have to let eternity show up *inside* of time. This takes work, but it's also ordinary. You probably already know what it feels like to let eternity show up inside of time.

Take an ordinary example. I'm busy. I'm rushing around at work, trying to catch up with grading I should have already finished. I feel bad about how I wasted time yesterday, and I'm worried, now, about not having enough time tomorrow. My attention is frazzled, stretched taut between regret for the past and worry about the future. Then a student stops by and interrupts me. I want to be done. I want to rest from this work and be done with time's demands. But, instead, Spirit intervenes. We make eye contact. I see her for the first time since she came in. I surrender. I *stop*. I pay attention. I listen to what the student is saying. I see what she needs. I offer my help. I forget about myself. I die. I let the end arrive early. Time continues to move, but now I'm not worried about time. A stillness takes hold at the heart of time's passage. Eternity has been stamped into time.

8

Shadows of
Things to Come

Hundreds of years before Christ was
born, Book of Mormon peoples lived
typologically. They lived as though their
salvation in Christ had already come.

Types are especially important in the Book of
Mormon. There, types are used to make sense of
the people's anticipatory experience of Christ.
Hundreds of years before his birth, they knew
about Christ, taught about Christ, and lived their
lives in Christ. How did they do this? How did
they live time out of order?

Like Alma, Book of Mormon prophets saw ordinances as the key to this new experience of time.
Their laws and rituals were important because, as
types, they invited Christ's future into their present. "There was a law given them," Abinadi says,
"a law of performances and of ordinances, a law
which they were to observe strictly from day to day,

to keep them in remembrance of God and their duty towards him. But behold, I say unto you, that all these things were types of things to come" (Mosiah 13:30–31).

Mormon makes this same point in Alma 25:15: "Notwithstanding the law of Moses, they did look forward to the coming of Christ, considering that the law of Moses was a type of his coming." In this verse, Mormon draws on language nearly identical to Alma 13. These ordinances, he says, are "a type of his coming" that showed the people how "to *look forward* to the coming of Christ." As types, these ordinances displayed a certain way of looking forward to the coming of Christ, a way that allowed them, even then, to share in Christ's life and resurrection.

But the Book of Mormon's clearest expression of this idea comes, as I mentioned in an earlier chapter, in the book of Jarom. Of Christ, Jarom says: "Wherefore, the prophets, and the priests, and the teachers, did labor diligently, exhorting with all long-suffering the people to diligence; teaching the law of Moses, and the intent for which it was given; persuading them to look forward unto the Messiah, and believe in him to come as though he already was" (Jarom 1:11). In this verse, instead of using the word *type*, Jarom gives a description of how types work. Nephite laws and ordinances were given by Christ with a certain intention: to persuade the people to "look forward" to the Messiah "and believe in him to come as though he already was."

The Book of Mormon is consistent on this point. Laws and ordinances aren't given for their own sake. Rather, they are given as types of Christ. And when people live these laws *as* types, they live time in a different way. They live in Christ as surely as if he had already come. But when these laws and ordinances are uprooted from Christ, when they aren't seen as types, they can do great harm. They can be—and commonly are—used as weapons for judging others and ourselves. In this vein, I may try to repurpose them as tools for leveraging praise or earning love or dismissing the poor. "I'm Christian *and you're not*. I keep the Word of Wisdom *and you don't*. I've paid my tithing or prepared my lesson or attended the temple, *and you haven't*." Done in the wrong way or for the wrong reasons, even good things sour. Jesus is relentless

> Laws and ordinances aren't given for their own sake. Rather, they are given as types of Christ.

in warning against this mishandling of the law. He calls it hypocrisy. "When thou prayest, thou shalt not be as the hypocrites are: for they love to pray standing in the synagogues and in the corners of the streets, that they may be seen of men. Verily I say unto you, They have their reward" (Matthew 6:5). Failing as types, severed from Christ, our laws and ordinances risk hypocrisy. They may yield some good, but they won't open onto a new life in Christ.

> Types reveal a different way— an already redeemed way—of being alive, of handling time and living God's law.

Types, then, are more than just symbols. *Types reveal a different way—an already redeemed way—of being alive, of handling time and living God's law.* Laws and ordinances then become powerful and life-giving.

Committed to the importance of types, the Book of Mormon doesn't just model what a Christian life looked like before Christ was born. It models what life in Christ will look like in any age. Reordering time, types allow us to die while we're still alive and to share in Christ's resurrection and redemption before we're dead. Our laws and ordinances may only partially overlap with those observed by the Lehites—we no longer live the law of Moses—but the need to see all laws and ordinances as types of Christ, as occasions for the intervention of his atoning power, is just as urgent.

9

Baptism Is a
Time Machine

Baptism is a type that reorders
our experience of time. Burying us
with Christ, baptism allows death
and redemption to arrive early.

Our own laws and ordinances as Latter-day Saints
are also types. In compressed, symbolic fashion,
they show us how to look forward to Christ in the
present. This is why both the Book of Mormon and
the New Testament focus on baptism. Baptism is
an exemplary type because it so plainly reorders
our experience of time.

I've touched on part of these verses before, but
Paul's description of baptism may be the best in all
of scripture. It rewards a closer look. Rather than
describing baptism as an act of ritual cleansing, he
describes it as a death and resurrection. I am buried
in the water and then raised from that death into
a new life.

Know ye not, that so many of us as were baptized into Jesus Christ were baptized into his death? Therefore we are buried with him by baptism into death: that like as Christ was raised up from the dead by the glory of the Father, even so we also should walk in newness of life. For if we have been planted together in the likeness of his death, we shall be also in the likeness of his resurrection: knowing this, that our old man is crucified with him, that the body of sin might be destroyed, that henceforth we should not serve sin. For he that is dead is freed from sin. Now if we be dead with Christ, we believe that we shall also live with him. (Romans 6:3–8)

Paul has no hope in anything but Christ. There is no hope here that, with a little more time, I could set my own life in order and get out from under the power of sin. Entangled in sin as I am, habitually looking forward in the wrong ways, there's only one exit: death. "He that is dead is freed from sin" (Romans 6:7). If death is the only way out of sin, Paul says, then let's get death over with. Instead of postponing my death and delaying the inevitable, baptism allows that death to arrive

37

early. Burying me in a watery grave, baptism allows me to die with Christ while I'm still alive. And then, having already crossed death's threshold, I can begin my resurrection in Christ before my own life has ended.

In this way, baptism is a time machine. It's a vehicle for atonement. As a type, baptism is a ritual engine for reordering my experience of time. It shuffles Christ's resurrected future into my mortal present and, in doing so, frees me from my sinful past.

As types, all ordinances are time machines. All of them invite us to live time out of order. With the sacrament each week, we anticipate in miniature the presence of God at that great wedding feast, the messianic banquet, promised at the end of time when "in this mountain shall the Lord of hosts make unto all people a feast of fat things," when "he will swallow up death in victory; and the Lord God will wipe away tears from off all faces" (Isaiah 25:6, 8). More, in the sacrament, Christ gives *himself* as that banquet's bread and wine. "I am the living bread which came down from heaven: if any

> As a type, baptism is a ritual engine for reordering my experience of time.

man eat of this bread, he shall live for ever: and the bread that I will give is my flesh, which I will give for the life of the world" (John 6:51). This messianic feast, impatient for the world to end, keeps breaking into the present every time we meet in Christ's name, say these prayers, and break this bread. In the same way, the endowment ceremony initiates us into a new way of handling time. Treating the whole of history as a series of types, it asks us to identify with Adam and Eve and practice living as though we, like them, had already passed through death's veil and into the presence of God.

> This messianic feast, impatient for the world to end, keeps breaking into the present every time we meet in Christ's name, say these prayers, and break this bread.

As a type, an ordinance is a door. This door is the end: the end of life, the end of time. But, because this end comes in the middle of life, in the present, a type is a door without a wall. Once I've passed through this door, I don't find myself in another world. I find myself right back where I started—but now with death already behind me. Having passed through the eye of a type, everything is just as it was and nothing will ever be the same.

I felt the weight of time when I was baptized. I was eight years old. I had reached the age of accountability. My father buried me in those waters, and, in a sense, he buried my childhood with me. From my baptism on, I felt like God was watching me. I felt like God was keeping score in a way that he hadn't before. Now if I did something wrong, I'd be guilty. Now I was on the hook. Now the law applied to me. The clock was ticking. In my mind, angels had been assigned, and they were keeping careful track of my many misdeeds. God's distance felt legally justified. Repentance, rather than being a name for how Christ was already at work in my life, already empowering and redeeming me, just felt like a form of court-mandated punishment.

No one told me what Paul said. No one told me that, by being baptized, I was dying and being resurrected. I was only told that, having been washed clean, I had better not get dirty again. This is good advice, but it's almost the opposite of what Paul describes. As an eight-year-old, I felt like my mortality *began* with my baptism. But Paul, instead, sees baptism as a way of bringing that mortality to an early *end*. He sees it as a way of putting death and sin behind me, right from the start, so that I can live in Christ here and now.

10

Fulfilling the Law in Christ

Christ fulfills the law. By living in Christ and "relying wholly upon the merits of him who is mighty to save," we can share in the law's fulfillment (2 Nephi 31:19).

The biggest difference that follows from this newly baptized way of handling time is a new relationship to the law. Outside of Christ, the law governs life. But once I've died and been resurrected with Christ, things are different. Rather than living under the law, I live in Christ. As Paul puts it, "for I through the law am dead to the law, that I might live unto God" (Galatians 2:19).

The Book of Mormon frequently pairs laws with ordinances as types. "There was a law given them," we've already seen Abinadi say, "a law of performances and of ordinances," and "all these things were types of things to come" (Mosiah 13:30, 31). Just like an ordinance, the law is a type.

As a type, the point of the law is Christ. And only Christ—defying, folding, and reordering time—can fulfill the law. All the rest of us "have sinned, and come short of the glory of God" (Romans 3:23). In fact, as "the Lamb slain from the foundation of the world," Christ's future work of redeeming the world and fulfilling the law was stamped into the world's own foundation (Revelation 13:8). From before the creation of the world, from the moment of its founding, it was as though Christ had already saved it. Salvation in Christ can appear right from time's beginning because Christ has "saved us, and called us with a holy calling, not according to our works, but according to his own purpose and grace, which was given us in Christ Jesus before the world began, but is now made manifest by the appearing of our Saviour Jesus Christ, who hath abolished death, and hath brought life and immortality to light through the gospel" (2 Timothy 1:9–10).

> As a type, the point of the law is Christ. And only Christ—defying, folding, and reordering time—can fulfill the law.

When God's laws are lived as types, as lessons in how to reorder my relationship to time, they connect me with life in Christ and the law's fulfillment. But when these laws come uncoupled from Christ—when I try to live these laws as an expression of ego, as a way of winning a prize, or in the same way that, lost and fallen, I naturally live time, from front to back, sequentially—then sin is the predictable outcome. Disjoined from Christ, I inevitably feel guilty and ashamed before the law. When this happens, the law breaks and "the commandment, which was ordained to life, I found to be unto death. For sin, taking an occasion by the commandment, deceived me, and by it slew me" (Romans 7:10–11). Without Christ, the fruit of the commandments is death rather than life. Without Christ, the law is partial and misleading. As Paul says, it "deceives" me rather than heals me. Without Christ, even my obedience sours into hypocrisy.

Laws are inherently chronological. They structure our experience of time. They outline, in advance, the connection between a present cause and a future effect, between a present action and a future consequence. A law says: if you do this in the present, then this will happen in the future. As a result, laws make it possible for

> Without laws, I would be blind to time and trapped in an empty present.

me to live looking forward. Without laws, I would be blind to time and trapped in an empty present. I *need* the law. I need the law to see what time is and how time works. But I *also* need Christ. In fact, the law itself needs Christ. Only Christ can fulfill the law. Does life in Christ destroy the law? No, but faith in Christ does fundamentally alter my relationship to that law. "Do we then make void the law through faith? God forbid: yea, we establish the law" (Romans 3:31).

With Christ, the law can channel and empower the works of love. In fact, laws are crucial to the work of love. I *must* learn obedience. But laws are also a temptation. They can tempt me into thinking that I don't—or, at least, *shouldn't*—need Christ. They can tempt me into thinking that if I could just be obedient enough on my own, then I wouldn't have to ask for help. If this were possible, then I could sidestep a relationship with God and worship an abstract law instead. I wouldn't have to rely "*wholly* upon the merits of him who is mighty to save" (2 Nephi 31:19, emphasis added). I could go around pretending that I'd earned all God's blessings and that God owed me his love. I could pretend that every blessing wasn't, at bottom, a gift. I could pretend, in fact, that with my obedience to the law I'd paid God back, perhaps even with interest. I could pretend that I'd earned my own salvation by way of the law. I wouldn't have to admit, as King Benjamin demands that I do, that it was God who "created you from the beginning, and is preserving you from day to day, by lending you breath, that ye may live and move and do according to your own will, and even supporting you from one moment to another" (Mosiah 2:21). I wouldn't have to admit that even "if ye should serve him with all your whole souls yet ye would be unprofitable servants" (Mosiah 2:21). The law, in this sense, is not just a blessing but a temptation.

> By revealing the consequences of my actions, the law may tempt me into looking beyond love's work in the present to focus, instead, on a promised reward.

But, even more fundamentally, the law can tempt me into *looking forward* in the wrong way. By revealing the consequences of my actions, the law may tempt me into looking beyond love's work in the present to focus, instead, on a promised reward. In this way, rather than waking me to a life in Christ, the law can lull me into dreaming about heavenly mansions. But love is not that kind of thing. Love is not a future reward promised in return for my present obedience. Love is a shared way of handling, in the present, all the blessings and troubles that inevitably accompany the passage of time. Love is the thing I'm looking for. But love isn't the *outcome* of my work, however noble that outcome. Love is Christ's *manner of doing* that work. Looking forward in the wrong way, I may miss—folded right into the present—the very thing I was looking for.

11

The Law as Love's Servant

As types of Christ, God's laws become
dead to me as life's master and, instead,
come alive in me as love's servant.

Once my resurrection is underway, it becomes obvious that what Christ said about the Sabbath is true about the law as a whole: "The sabbath was made for man, and not man for the sabbath: therefore the Son of man is Lord also of the sabbath" (Mark 2:27–28). Christ is the Lord even of the law. The law was made for the sake of a life in Christ, not life in Christ for the sake of fulfilling the law.

Nephi describes how types changed his own relationship to the law. "And, notwithstanding we believe in Christ, we keep the law of Moses, and look forward with steadfastness unto Christ, until the law shall be fulfilled. For, for this end was the law given; wherefore the law hath become dead unto us, and we are made alive in Christ because of our faith; yet we keep the law because of the commandments" (2 Nephi 25:24–25). In Christ, Nephi relates to the law as a type. Christ is the end for which the law was given. And because Christ's future has already been superimposed on his present, Nephi experiences time as folded or layered. For him, there is a wrinkle in time's line that sets both present and future side by side. As a result, he says, "the law hath become dead unto us, *and* we are made alive in Christ."

> "The law hath become dead unto us, *and* we are made alive in Christ because of our faith" (2 Nephi 25:25).

Paul develops an analogy along these same lines. Paul urges me to be crucified with Christ because "the law hath dominion over a man as long as he liveth" (Romans 7:1). The law has dominion over me only as long as I'm alive. The law, apart from Christ, dominates my experience of time. It commands things to happen in their prescribed order. First life, then death. First the present, then the future. First obedience, then (later) redemption.

Paul compares the law to an overbearing husband who insists that life be lived according to his own house rules. In such a case it's true that "the woman which hath a husband is bound by the law to her husband so long as he liveth; but if the husband be dead, she is loosed from the law of her husband" (Romans 7:2). As long as he's alive, she's bound to him. But, if the husband dies, she's free. This is exactly how Nephi describes the law. Nephi still keeps the law, but the law doesn't own him. The law no longer dominates his experience of time. "The law," Nephi says, has—just like this woman's husband—"become dead unto us" (2 Nephi 25:25).

The good news, Paul claims, is that "if her husband be dead, she is free from that law; so that she is no adulteress, though she be married to another man" (Romans 7:3). With her husband dead, she is free to marry again. And Paul already has another suitor in mind: Christ. This time, he urges, marry for love. "Wherefore, my brethren, ye also are become dead to the law by the body of Christ; that ye should be married to another, even to him who is raised from the dead" (Romans 7:4). Paul, of course, is *not* suggesting that I abandon the law. *Do not misunderstand this: if I abandon the law, I've lost the type and, with it, my connection to Christ.* Rather, he's arguing, as Nephi did, that my relationship to the law must be reordered. The law, instead of playing the role of the domineering husband, must itself die and become a servant. The law, instead of promising death, must serve the ends of a life in Christ. Christ is the Lord, not the law. Christ is the Master. He is the King of kings.

This is important to see. Like an ordinance, the law is a type. As a type, the law is no longer about itself. The law is about Christ. The law becomes dead to me as life's master and, instead, comes alive *in* me as love's servant. And, crucially, instead of experiencing life in terms of my guilt before the law, I now experience the law in terms of my responsibility for life. Shame and fear—unlike weakness, failure, and responsibility—are not part of a life in Christ.

> The law, instead of promising death, must serve the ends of a life in Christ.

This difference is felt at least as much as it is understood. In Christ, my relationship to the law *feels* very different. Alive in Christ, I still feel compelled by the law to love others and be responsible for life. But this imperative to love no longer feels like a judgment. It no longer takes the shape of a condemnation of my life by the law. And then, because the law no longer presents itself in the form of a condemnation, because the law's regard for me is itself now felt as an *expression* of Christ's love, I find myself empowered rather than punished by the law. The law, as love's servant, empowers me to roll up my sleeves and do love's work. Rather than working to secure God's perfect love in the distant future, I go to work right now in a manner that displays God's love as a gift already superimposed on the present. I stop doing tacit cost/benefit analyses, weighing the pros and cons of keeping or breaking the law. I don't ask myself if praying today or going to church this week or doing my home teaching this month will get me what I want in the future, either in the short term (rest and fun) or the long term (happiness and heaven). Instead, I do these things for their own sake out of love. I forget myself.

> Because the law no longer presents itself in the form of a condemnation, because the law's regard for me is itself now felt as an expression of Christ's love, I find myself empowered rather than punished by the law.

In this way, the law is like water. There is no life without water. I *have* to have water. I have to learn how to keep the law. But without Christ, the law works against itself. It works against life. It freezes solid. Without Christ, the law turns to ice and traps me in sin. Frozen, I die. Only as a type of Christ, only as a servant of Christ's love, does the law thaw. Christ is not only the life and light of the whole world. He is the life and light of the law.

12

Christ Is the End of Every Law

Paul and the Book of Mormon often focus on the law of Moses as a type of Christ. But all laws, not just the law of Moses, are types of Christ.

When talking about the law, both Paul and the Book of Mormon focus on the law of Moses. The law of Moses, they argue, is about Christ. It is a type meant to show people how to look forward to Christ's coming and live as though he were already present. However, because they focus on the law of Moses, it is sometimes assumed that what Paul and the Book of Mormon say about the law applies *only* to the law of Moses. For my part, I think this is too narrow.

I think it makes more sense to see every gospel law, not just the law of Moses, as a type of Christ, grounded from the start in the priority of his love.

In both Paul's writings and the Book of Mormon, it makes more sense to read the law of Moses as one *example* of how the law, in general, works. And, especially, I think it makes more sense to see every gospel law, not just the law of Moses, as a type of Christ, grounded from the start in the priority of his love. The basics of religion—like the basics of life—are the same whether I'm waiting for Christ's first coming or his second. This is why both the New Testament and the Book of Mormon are still so powerful. The Book of Mormon, in particular, is intended for us. We are like them. Our problems are the same. And life in Christ is the same. Like the law of Moses, baptism is still clearly intended to function as a type of Christ. Like the law of Moses, our laws can still do great harm when they aren't grounded in Christ. And, as with the law of Moses, Christ still wants us to live in his presence, both in the next life and in this one. Some of their laws and ordinances are different from ours, but all of these laws and ordinances, past or present, are types of Christ that open onto a new experience of time where our redemption is no longer postponed.

Consider Paul's most important letter, his letter to the Romans. There, Paul's account of the law constantly overlaps with his discussion of the law of Moses. But, too, Paul's way of talking consistently shows that he has something deeper in mind than just that Jewish law.

For instance, Paul's audience is Roman. Some of his audience may have been Jewish or, at one time, converts to Judaism, but many of them were Gentiles. Paul, though, clearly sees his descriptions of the law as applying to both Jews and Gentiles. He even claims that Gentiles who don't know anything about the ritual details of the law of Moses—details like circumcision—can live the law "by nature" and even "fulfil the law" better than those who *do* know its ritual details (Romans 2:27). "If the uncircumcision keep the righteousness of the law, shall not his uncircumcision be counted for circumcision? . . . For he is not a Jew, which is one outwardly; neither is that circumcision, which is outward in the flesh: but he is a Jew, which is one inwardly; and circumcision is that of the heart" (Romans 2:26, 28–29). How is this possible? How could Gentiles who have never heard of Moses still know the law and fulfill it? Because, Paul says, God's law is manifest in life itself: "For the invisible things of him from the creation of the world are clearly seen, being understood by the things that are made" (Romans 1:20). Because the cause-and-effect structure of the law is written in life's own bones, the law is obvious in even the most ordinary experience of time. Even without a special revelation, people intuitively know that it's wrong to lie, steal, and murder. Mosaic rituals may officially trace the shape of these laws and display them as types of Christ, but the law is openly revealed to the whole world in "the things that are made," in the substance of creation itself.

Notice, too, that when Paul uses examples of broken laws, he uses ethical rather than ritual examples. That is, the law Paul *primarily* has in mind is the moral law, summarized in the ten commandments. When he gives a laundry list of broken laws in Romans 1:21–31 or Romans 3:10–18, all of the named laws are ethical rather than ritual: idolatry, murder, adultery, deceit, covetousness, envy, theft, etc. And these moral laws, unlike the ritual elements of the law of Moses, remain firmly in force for Christians. When Paul talks about becoming "dead to the law

> When Paul talks about becoming "dead to the law by the body of Christ," he is describing a fundamental change in our relation to the law as a whole and to the moral law in particular (Romans 7:4).

by the body of Christ," he is describing a fundamental change in our relation to the law as a whole and to the moral law in particular (Romans 7:4). This change turns on adopting a new relationship to time that, rather than abandoning the law, finally allows that law to be fulfilled in Christ. As a general rule, it seems that what Paul and Nephi say about the law also applies to laws today.

13

Law and the Problem of Desire

Laws and desires are intertwined. They are intertwined by time. Learning how to handle time in a different way means learning how to handle both laws and desires in a new way.

Consider one additional example of how Paul treats the law as something that runs deeper than just the law of Moses. Consider Paul's famous discussion in Romans 7:7–25 of how desire is shaped by the law.

In these verses, Paul argues that the connection between law and desire is both universal and straightforward: I want what I lack. The law shapes desire by showing me what I don't have. And, especially, the law shows me what I *don't* have by telling me what I *can't* have. The law can enflame desire for something just by forbidding it. I didn't even know what I wanted before I couldn't have it. This kind of thinking is especially obvious with children or if you've ever tried to diet. "For I had not known lust," Paul says, "except the law had said, Thou shalt not covet" (Romans 7:7). By drawing a line in the sand, the law entices me to cross it. "What shall we say then? Is the law sin? God forbid. Nay, I had not known sin, but by the law" (v. 7).

This connection between law and desire is a basic part of human experience. And this connection between law and desire has, of course, to do with my experience of time. When I handle time in the wrong way, when I look forward in the wrong manner, I also end up handling the law in the wrong way.

Law and desire are tied together because the law orders my experience of time. The law bridges the present and the future, connecting causes with effects and actions with consequences. But, for this very reason, law and desire go hand in hand. Law and desire are tied together because desire is itself a certain way of looking forward. In general, desire is a way of looking forward to what I don't have. Desire is a way of looking forward that frames my present in terms of the future's *absence*. When I think about my job, I don't

> Desire is a way of looking forward that frames my present in terms of the future's *absence*.

60

think about the job I have, I think about the job I don't yet have. When I zip down the freeway, I don't think about the car I have, but the car I don't yet have. When I step into my closet, I see all the clothes that don't quite fit or match, not the ones that do. When I reflect on my life, I don't see the good that I've done but the mounting ways in which I've failed. Full of desire, I see what's absent. Desire halos everything I see with an image of what it is not, with a shadow of what I lack or what I would have preferred, with a dreamy future that isn't this ordinary present. These shadows are especially common—and dangerous—when it comes to the people closest to me. Absorbed in desire, I don't see them as they are, I see them in terms of what they are not. Law and desire must be handled with care. I have to watch, as Paul warns, for how the law itself helps generate these shadows as a by-product of what it predicts and forbids (cf. Romans 7:7–11).

It's this connection between law and desire that, as Paul points out, makes the law vulnerable to being co-opted by sin. Sin, taking advantage of how the law fuels and conditions desire, "taking occasion by the commandment, wrought in me all manner of concupiscence" (Romans 7:8). On one level, sin is a problem because it breaks the law. But, at a deeper level, at the level of the heart, sin is a problem because it can *hijack* the law and then wield the law as a weapon against the possibility of love. As a sinner, I can get trapped by desire and separated from God because, abusing the law, I look forward in the wrong way. Living outside of Christ, I get trapped in the law and live time wrongly.

What does it look like to look forward in the wrong way? What does it look like to desire in the wrong way? When I desire in the wrong way, I fail to love things for their own sake. I fail to love them for what they actually are. I want them only as a means to satisfying my own hungers and solving my own problems. When I want things in the wrong way, I invest them with an imaginary power to give me something they can't. I invest them with the power to save me. In cases like this, I may want a new coat or a new car or new job, but I want them *because I hope that they could finally fill the hole in my heart.*

> At a deeper level, at the level of the heart, sin is a problem because it can hijack the law and then wield the law as a weapon against the possibility of love.

62

I want them as antidotes to the trouble and vulnerability of time. There's nothing inherently wrong with a new coat, a new car, or a new job. But these things can't save me. And they certainly can't save me from time. It's the essence of sin to act as if they could. In this same way, not even the law can save me. If I relate to the law as an object of desire, if I relate to the law as if the law itself could save me, then I'll end up holding the law in the wrong way. I'll end up asking the law to do something that it can't. And when this doesn't work—as it won't—I'll be angry and ashamed. The law can't save me. Only Christ can save me.

In order to begin a new life in Christ, I must die to the law and look forward to the future in a new way. I must look forward to Christ as already given. I must learn to live time—and, thus, desire—differently. I must learn to *feel* both time and desire differently. Desire, like the law, must die to me as life's master so that it can live in me as love's servant.

This doesn't mean that I stop experiencing desire. And it certainly doesn't mean that desire is bad. Without desire, I would have no life for Christ to resurrect. There is no love without law, and there is no life without desire. But it does mean that

I have to learn to live my desires, like laws and ordinances, as types. Desire, as a way of looking forward, must learn to look forward to Christ. And, specifically, desire must learn to look forward to Christ *as though he had already come.* In Christ, I can both feel desire and be at peace. I can be alive and enter the rest of the Lord. I can live both the present and the future. When I live my desires as types of Christ, there is a perfect calm at the heart of those desires, a deep stillness at the center of my striving. This stillness isn't afraid and it isn't guilty. It isn't scared about how things will turn out and it isn't ashamed about what I lack. By fulfilling the law, Christ forever changes my relationship to the law. And by fulfilling desire, Christ forever changes my relationship to my desires.

14

Love Is Christ's Manner of Looking Forward

Love is the key to fulfilling the law because it names a new way of handling time.

To say that the law can only be fulfilled by Christ is to say that the law can only be fulfilled by love. Love is the point of the law. "All the law and the prophets" hang on this imperative to love (Matthew 22:40). Without love, the law comes unplugged from Christ. It stops functioning as a type and leaves me hopeless. When, instead of love, the law generates fear, anger, guilt, envy, and frustration, then the law is broken. A loveless law is a broken law. A loveless law is a law incapable of mercy *or* justice. A loveless law is an occasion for selfishness, pride, and hypocrisy.

Love is the key to life in Christ because love is itself a certain way of handling time. Love is a certain way of looking forward, a way of looking at the world, right now, as already redeemed. Love is a way of looking at this fragile world as already beset, on a global scale, by an early resurrection.

Full of love, I die while I'm still alive. I lose my life before I'm dead, and, then, in Christ, I find it. Love works just as Christ said: "He that findeth his life shall lose it: and he that loseth his life for my sake shall find it" (Matthew 10:39). Love is hard because it's a kind of death. To love, I have to be willing to die. I have to be willing to let go of my life and give myself to caring for the lives of others. And, then, to continually live *in* love, I have to be willing to die every day, every hour, in ways that are big and small, again and again. I yield on the freeway. I bite my tongue when I want to criticize. I put down what I'm doing and read to my kids. I stay up late and finish the dishes. I get up early and drive my daughter to seminary. I grade the next paper. I put on my running shoes. I exhale. I surrender my life. Crucified with Christ, I practice surrendering all day long until my days are filled with the rest of the Lord. I practice dying

> Love is a way of looking at this fragile world as already beset, on a global scale, by an early resurrection.

as a way of life. And I keep practicing until I find the kind of rest that comes only from living my life in the form of a thousand daily deaths.

Paul is uncompromising on this point. There are many spiritual gifts. And there are many laws that promise blessings. But, without love, they're all empty. "Though I speak with the tongues of men and of angels, and have not charity, I am become as sounding brass, or a tinkling cymbal" (1 Corinthians 13:1). And the same is true with other gifts like prophecy, knowledge, and faith: "And though I have the gift of prophecy, and understand all mysteries, and all knowledge; and though I have all faith, so that I could remove mountains, and have not charity, I am nothing" (v. 2). Even my good works, my obedience and self-sacrifice—even these are hollow without love: "And though I bestow all my goods to feed the poor, and though I give my body to be burned, and have not charity, it profiteth me nothing" (v. 3). Everything but love will fail. Everything but love, defying time in Christ, will pass away. Only "charity never faileth: but whether there be prophecies, they shall fail; whether there be tongues, they shall cease; whether there be knowledge, it shall vanish away" (v. 8).

The law is no different. The law is a gift. But the law, like all these other gifts, will also find an end in Christ. Love never will. Unlike love, the law is no lord or master. Take, for instance, the difference between guilt and responsibility. Apart from Christ—ungrounded in love, postponing resurrection—the law *does* pose as my master.

Mastered by the law, I stand guilty before it. I'm judged and condemned. Guilty before the law, I'm cut off. I'm isolated in my weakness. I'm more alone, less connected, and even less able to love. Loveless, I'm nothing. But responsibility is different. Grounded in love, the law doesn't condemn my weakness, it empowers me to be responsible *for* that weakness. Rooted in Christ, the law doesn't isolate me from others, it binds me to them. It urges me to care for them. It helps me to be responsible to them. In Christ, the law holds me responsible by empowering me to respond to the hurt I've caused and the needs others have.

> Grounded in love, the law doesn't condemn my weakness, it empowers me to be responsible for that weakness.

Love is a useful measure for distinguishing guilt from responsibility. Guilt is about me. It centers me on myself and weakens my power to care for myself and for other people. But responsibility faces the opposite direction. Responsibility is an act of love. It recognizes wrongdoing and repents of it. But rather than acting penitent out of fear or shame, it lets those self-centered feelings be crucified with Christ. Then, alive in Christ rather than in myself, I become capable of responding—even to my own weakness—with love.

But if I haven't died, the law will remain my master. I'll always feel guilty. I'll always feel inadequate and ashamed. I'll always be thinking about myself when I fail to meet the law's measures, and worrying about myself will leave me feeling more alone. But if, in love, I've died early, then everything is different. When I inevitably fall short, I won't feel guilty—"I" am already dead. Instead, resurrected in Christ, I'll take responsibility. I'll become capable of mercy and justice. I'll take my weakness as another occasion to care for the lives that we share.

15

The Yoke of Christ

Alive in Christ, I put down life's burden
and take up Christ's yoke. This burden
is my future. This yoke is Christ's love.

Love's peculiar way of looking forward is liberating. If the future has already arrived, then I can put down that burden. I can find rest. "Come unto me, all ye that labour and are heavy laden, and I will give you rest. Take my yoke upon you, and learn of me; for I am meek and lowly in heart: and ye shall find rest unto your souls. For my yoke is easy, and my burden is light" (Matthew 11:28–30). This is true, but what is my heavy burden? What weighs me down and keeps me from entering the rest of the Lord? This burden is, I think, time. This burden is the *future*, manifest in the present as guilt, fear, stress, lust, envy, and resentment. And the weight of that future, of a perpetually postponed redemption, is crushing. When I lie in bed and close my eyes, I can feel it. I can feel time's weight. It squats like an anvil on my chest. I can feel the creep of a cell-deep panic at the thought of what I haven't done, at the thought of what I haven't become, at the thought of what I don't have, at the thought of all that eludes me.

Notice this about time. My obsession with myself is largely an obsession with my future. I identify myself with my future. Will I be happy? Will I get the girl? Will I win the game? Will I get the job? Will I be loved and praised? Will I be saved? All of these questions are framed in the future tense. And, framed in the future tense, all of them invite worry and fear. This kind of worry and fear draws me out of the present and obscures the truth about Christ and about love. They invite me to hope in something other than Christ. They refuse to live in Christ as though he had already come. They prevent me from entering the rest of the Lord.

> My obsession with myself is largely an obsession with my future.

Christ offers something different. He invites me to come to him. He invites me to put down my burden. What I'm doing is no way to live. It's no

71

way to handle time. It's no way to look forward. It's lonely and worried. It's frustrated and angry. Christ invites me to watch him and learn from him. He invites me to take up time's yoke the way he does: by being meek and lowly in heart. Like Christ, I need to practice death as a way of life and, thus, press death into the service of life.

This is counterintuitive. My intuition is to post-pone death, not embrace it. My intuition is to stick to my own plan and live time chronologically, to live the present as a means of winning a future that could save me. My intuition is to love the present in light of what I hope the present will eventually become. In this way, I'm seduced into aiming right through the present—right through the people I'm with, through the work I'm doing, through the place where I stand—at the promised outcome. As a result, my way of looking *forward* ends up being a way of looking *through*. Love may look forward to things, but it doesn't look through them. Love locks eyes with them. Love sees them, right here, right as they are, right now: ugly and beautiful, strong and weak, whole

> Love, rather than living time as a means to an end, lives time as an end in itself.

and maimed, sinner and saint. Love, primed by Spirit, cares for them as they are.

Love, rather than living time as a means to an end, lives time as an end in itself. If I've already died—if the end has already come—then work is not just a means to some other end. With my own end already passed, everything becomes an end in itself. Everything becomes valuable in its own right, on its own terms, in its own present weakness. In Christ, I learn to love life for its own sake. Because I'm already dead, I'm free to "give to every man that asketh" (Luke 6:30). I can let things go. I can give things away. And, especially, I'm free to treat others the way I want to be treated. I'm free to treat them as ends in themselves, not just as means to something else. "As ye would that men should do to you, do ye also to them likewise" (Luke 6:31). I can treat them as being worth my time and attention, as ends in themselves, because my own end has, in Christ, already come and gone.

I put down my burden and take up Christ's yoke. This burden is the future. This yoke is love. But this yoke is light because yokes are, by definition, shared. No longer holding life at arm's length, no longer aiming through this world at another, I'm also no longer alone. Not only am I yoked with Christ, I'm yoked by Christ's love with the whole of this present world. Yoked in Christ with the world, we pull together.

16

God's Promises Fold the Future into the Present

Paul sees Abraham as a model for understanding the relationship between Christ and the law. God promises Abraham a child. Abraham has faith in this promise and lives in Christ as though that future had already come.

As the end of the law, love runs deeper than the law. And, in the same way, Christ runs deeper than time. Whenever Paul talks about the law, he leads it back to love. And whenever he talks about time, he leads it back to Christ. Paul is keenly aware of how the law is grounded in Christ. He's keenly aware of how abstract principles are grounded in real people. Laws are made for people, not people for laws. Laws grow out of relationships. They give needed

> Laws are made for people, not people for laws. Laws grow out of relationships.

shape to those relationships, but laws don't run as deep as the relationships they brace.

In this respect, Paul takes Abraham as a model for understanding the relationship between Christ and the law. In Paul's account, Abraham receives a law, but the law doesn't save him. Abraham is alive in Christ because he's faithful to a promise that *precedes* the law. "What shall we say then that Abraham our father . . . hath found?" (Romans 4:1). Did Abraham work through the law to earn God's blessing? No, Paul says. "For if Abraham were justified by works, he hath whereof to glory" (v. 2). Then how was the promise made? "What saith the scripture? Abraham believed God, and it was counted unto him for righteousness" (v. 3, cf. Genesis 15:6). But what did Abraham believe? Abraham received a promise, and he received it in good faith. He "staggered not at the promise of God" (Romans 4:20). He trusted God's promise. This promise is often referred to as the "Abrahamic covenant." In short—and I will return to this— Abraham is promised that he would be the "father of many nations" and that his descendants would help save the whole human family, both Israelites and Gentiles (v. 17). Because this promise involves God's work of saving and sealing all the world's families, "therefore it is of faith, that it might be by grace; to the end the promise might be sure to all the seed; not to that only which is of the law, but to that also which is of the faith of Abraham; who is the father of us all" (v. 16).

What role, then, did laws and ordinances play? Laws and ordinances were given later, Paul says, after the promise was received and believed, as "a *seal* of the righteousness of the faith which he had" (Romans 4:11, emphasis added). These laws and ordinances serve the ends of love, but they don't, in themselves, save Abraham. Rather, Christ saves Abraham. With a promise, Christ bound himself to Abraham. And, trusting this promise, Abraham was bound in relationship to Christ. Then, in light of this promise, Abraham, like Nephi and Alma, lived in Christ as though he had already come.

The gospel is a promise and God's promises aren't bound by time. Promises defy time. They bring the future into the present. Promises are a certain way of looking forward. When I promised myself to my wife, I didn't just bind myself to her in the present. I gave her my future. Without waiting for that future to arrive, without waiting to see what sorrows or joys would come, I promised. Dressed in white, we knelt at an altar in the temple and joined hands. We were terribly young. The mirrors, set face to face, reflected endless futures at which we couldn't guess. Still, I loved her. I gave her all those futures as a gift. And we kissed. Now, promised to each other and sealed by a holy ordinance, we live as though those futures had already come. Now, in a very real way, our futures are already given as gifts in the present. And, now, we're empowered by those promises to love each other in the present.

But even if I've managed, today, to fold time with a promise and give my future to my wife in the present, that doesn't mean I won't need to do the same tomorrow. This is not a onetime event. In Christ, time persists. But, promised to each other in Christ, time is now a yoke we can share. I don't have to do this alone. I don't have to love alone. By loving me, my wife makes room for me to love her. And by loving her, I make room for her to love me. Our individual ideas about the future, centered on ourselves, may go their separate ways, but we can always meet in the present just as we are.

> Love, folding time like a type, takes the shape of a promise.

Love, folding time like a type, takes the shape

of a promise. And these promises, by making the future present, transfigure my experience of the present. The present feels different when the future arrives early. The present feels different when the future is already promised. It has a different quality. It unfolds at a different pace. It bears a different set of responsibilities.

In Christ, the future is given as though it had already come. There's no reason to rush. There's no reason to fear. There's no reason to feel ashamed. There's no cause for brushing other people aside as I hurry someplace else. There's room in the present for each thing to have its season. There's room for agency and creativity. There's room for Spirit. There's space to breathe. There's time for love.

17

Faith, Repentance, Baptism, and the Gift of the Holy Ghost

We exercise faith in Christ by trusting God's promise. We surrender our futures and die to our pasts by practicing repentance. The baptismal ordinance seals this promise and shows us how to look forward to Christ as though he had already returned. And then, without waiting, the Spirit stamps the shape of a life in God's presence directly into the substance of our mortal lives.

Obedience is a good name for my response to a law. But faith is a much better name for my response to a person. Especially, faith is a better name for my response to the promise of another person's love. Faith follows love. I need to keep faith with Christ's love, and I need to be faithful to the promise of love that binds us.

Just as Christ's promise is deeper than the law, faith is deeper than compliance. If I don't greet Christ's promise with faith—if I don't trust that he can promise the future and, thus, give that future now—then no amount of obedience can bring me into his presence. If my obedience isn't grounded in faith, then I won't be aiming for Christ, I'll be aiming at the law. But without faith, even if I hit the law, I'll miss Christ.

It's obvious that faith must come first. Faith is the first principle. "We believe that the first principles and ordinances of the Gospel are: first, Faith in the Lord Jesus Christ; second, Repentance; third, Baptism by immersion for the remission of sins; fourth, Laying on of hands for the gift of the Holy Ghost" (Articles of Faith 1:4). In order to live in Christ, I don't need faith in an abstract law, I need "faith *in the Lord Jesus Christ*." I have to begin where Abraham began: not with the law, "for if they which are of the law be heirs, faith is made void, and the promise made of none effect" (Romans 4:14). Rather, I have to begin with the promise because the promise "is of faith, that it might be by grace" (Romans 4:16). The law can and must work hand in hand with Christ's promise, but it can't substitute for that promise.

> Just as Christ's promise is deeper than the law, faith is deeper than compliance.

Repentance works along the same lines. Repentance, like faith, is personal. Where guilt and shame may be good names for how I feel when measured by the law, repentance names my willingness to change and be responsible in light of Christ's committed love. Repentance, like faith, is grounded in a relationship. It's grounded in the promise that seals this relationship. In Hebrew, the word for repentance (*shuv*) also means, among other things, "to turn." When I repent, I turn around. I stop facing the wrong direction. I stop looking forward in the wrong way. I stop looking *through* things and, instead, I start to see them. And this power to be sensitive and respond—this power to be responsible—is the key to repentance. It's the key to being alive. Repenting, I let my old self die. I take up repentance as a way of practicing death, moment by moment, for the sake of life.

Baptism is the gate. As a type, it marks my formal surrender, my willingness to die early. It introduces me to a Christian way of looking forward. Baptism is the mold into which my repentance is poured. It shapes my impulse to repent into a new way of handling time. My relationships to both my past and future change. Repentant, my past no longer owns me. And, repentant, the future no longer mortgages my present. Rather than being a slave to my past mistakes or future expectations, the past and future become servants of my present life.

These are the basics. First, I trust in Christ's promise. Second, I turn back toward the present with a sense of responsibility. Third, without waiting for the next life, baptism formally stamps eternity into time. And then, fourth, I begin to share in Christ's life and resurrection by way of the Spirit. I'm given the gift of the Holy Ghost. The gift of the Spirit is a kind of down payment on eternal life. "He which stablisheth us with you in Christ," Paul says, "and hath anointed us, is God; who hath also sealed us, and given *the earnest* of the Spirit in our hearts" (2 Corinthians 1:21–22, emphasis added). The gift of the Spirit, Paul says, is like the "earnest" money that seals an agreement (like a down payment on a new home) and makes that promise binding. By superimposing a life in God's presence onto these mortal bodies, the Spirit seals God's promise and makes that promise binding. The Spirit is God's way of giving right now what he has also promised to give later: a life with him.

I remember, with vivid clarity, just one part of

my baptism. I remember my confirmation. My father gave the blessing. He placed his hands on my head and prayed. I remember the feeling of his hands on my head as he commanded me to receive the Holy Ghost. My head was small. His hands were big. His hands were warm and surprisingly heavy. And if I had felt worried or alone before my baptism, I didn't feel that way now. I felt connected. I felt alive. His hands on my head felt like God's promise, already kept.

> The Spirit is God's way of giving right now what he has also promised to give later: a life with him.

18

The Body of Christ Has Many Members

Life in Christ is shared, not just with Christ but with other people. It is impossible to be alive in Christ alone.

None of this works without the Holy Ghost. Spirit is the lifeblood of the body of Christ. Buried with Christ, I'm resurrected with Christ. Giving up my own life, dying to my own future, I become part of Christ's present resurrection. I become part of the body of Christ. But this body isn't my own. It's Christ's. And, like his yoke, this body is shared. This body offers a new kind of life, a common life, a life lived outside of myself, a life that is broken like bread and shared like wine.

Still, though we share this life in Christ, we're not all the same. As a whole, the body of Christ possesses all the gifts of the Spirit, but no one person has every gift. Our different gifts make us different. "To one is given by the Spirit the word of wisdom; to another the word of knowledge by the same Spirit; to another faith by the same Spirit; to another the gifts of healing by the same Spirit; to another the working of miracles; to another prophecy; to another discerning of spirits; to another divers kinds of tongues; to another the interpretation of tongues: but all these worketh that one and the self-same Spirit, dividing to every man severally as he will" (1 Corinthians 12:8–11). I'm encouraged to seek every gift. But, at least for now, I share in all these gifts only by sharing in the body of Christ.

I'm encouraged to seek every gift. But, at least for now, I share in all these gifts only by sharing in the body of Christ.

I lack many gifts, and many of the gifts I do have are not the gifts I wanted. My gifts may be backward and small—I wanted to know but instead I can listen, I wanted to see angels but instead I'm nearsighted, I wanted to heal but instead I can mourn—but Spirit can still flow through them. And by refusing to hide even these small gifts, by openly allowing my own plans for the future to be superseded, I can share in these other gifts now.

The temptation is to think I could do this

alone. Or that I could live this resurrection just with Christ, just the two of us. But the body of Christ is not one, or even two. The body of Christ is many. "For as the body is one, and hath many members, and all the members of that one body, being many, are one body: so also is Christ" (1 Corinthians 12:12). The foot can't say: if I'm not the hand I wanted to be, then I'm not part of Christ's body. The bowels can't say: if I can't pump blood like the heart, then I'm not part of Christ's body. The nose can't say: if I can't see like the eye, then I'm not part of Christ's body. Nor the other way around. "The eye cannot say unto the hand, I have no need of thee: nor again the head of the feet, I have no need of you. Nay, *much more those members of the body, which seem to be more feeble, are necessary*; and those members of the body, which we think to be less honourable" (1 Corinthians 12:21–23, emphasis added). All the parts of the body are needed, even those that are less honorable and less beautiful.

I may admire strength and want to be strong, but in Christ I find a divine weakness. My new life depends on sharing this weakness. Those who are "less honorable" or those who "seem to be more feeble" are, Paul says, "necessary." But if I use the law mainly as a tool for measuring the weakness of my fellow members, then I'll despise that weakness. And, more, if I despise their weakness, I will also despise my own.

In one of my first areas as a missionary, I knew an elder who seemed "feeble" and "less honorable." Part of me despised him. He didn't seem very smart. He didn't appear very handsome. He wore the wrong kind of shoes. He was awkward. He didn't know the scriptures. He couldn't approach a door. I was not impressed. If we went on splits, I was embarrassed. Rather than loving him, I used the law to measure and dismiss him. Then, one morning, I was laid low. We were tracting, and I was hit between the eyes by a thought that was emphatically not my own: "This elder you despise already bears the stamp of God's image. If you can't see it, then you don't know the first thing about God." And it was true. My heart broke and I looked again and it was obviously true. The image of God was already engraved on his countenance (cf. Alma 5:19).

In the body of Christ our weakness is an occasion for care rather than judgment. The body of Christ isn't strong because it has no weaknesses. The body of Christ is strong because it's the place where weakness is shared. And our weakness, our need for each other, is the very thing that seals this sharing. When I live in Christ, things get turned upside down. The end arrives at the beginning. The last becomes first. The greatest become the least, and the least become types of Christ. In Christ, we're all bound together. If "one member suffer, all the members suffer with it" (1 Corinthians 12:26).

In the body of Christ our weakness is an occasion for care rather than judgment.

19

The Hearts of the Fathers

As we live in Christ, our selfishness dies and we live outside of ourselves. Instead of just keeping life for our own use, we share it with those nearest to us, especially our families.

The plain truth is that "we without them cannot be made perfect; neither can they without us be made perfect" (D&C 128:18). Redemption is a family affair. To be alive is to be intertwined with other lives. To be given a gift is to depend on other people's gifts. This is true in every world. It's true on earth and it's true in heaven. "That same sociality which exists among us here will exist among us there" (D&C 130:2). Dying to sin and living in Christ means dying to the fantasy that life need not be shared. It means dying

> Dying to sin and living in Christ means dying to the fantasy that life need not be shared.

to the fantasy that I could ever be whole on my own.

This is where Elijah comes in. Elijah is the bearer of this promise. "Before the coming of the great and dreadful day of the Lord," Malachi says, Christ "will send you Elijah the prophet" (Malachi 4:5). As a prophet, Elijah is sent with a specific job. His job is to come early—before the great and dreadful day of the Lord, before the world ends— to show me the end of the world. If I can't learn to see this end before it happens, if I'm too afraid to die early, then Christ will "smite the earth with a curse" and this curse will burn me up and leave me "neither root nor branch" (Malachi 4:6, 1). If I reject God's promise and keep postponing the end until the end, I'll live my whole life alone, rootless and branchless.

Elijah's job is to prevent this. His job is to "turn the heart of the fathers to the children, and the heart of the children to their fathers" (Malachi 4:6). His job is to fold time like a fan so that each generation touches, in the present, both the past and the future. Elijah folds time by turning hearts. I need him to announce Christ because my heart is facing the wrong direction. My heart is looking forward in the wrong way. Rather than facing toward others, my heart is turned away.

It's the same problem with every generation. Delivering the law, Moses says: "See, I have set before thee this day life and good, and death and evil; in that I command thee this day to love the Lord thy God, to walk in his ways, and to keep his commandments" (Deuteronomy 30:15–16). But, he warns, if I don't, "if thine heart turn away, so that thou wilt not hear, but shalt be drawn away, and worship other gods, and serve them," then I will suffer Malachi's curse (Deuteronomy 30:17).

If, today, I turn my heart to God, I will live. The trouble, though, is that my heart keeps turning away from today. And, as a result, my heart keeps turning away from God. Instead, my heart keeps getting "led astray" by other gods. I keep running after idols in the future. I keep looking forward in the wrong manner. I keep hoping to be saved by something other than Christ. But these other gods can't save me. Unlike Christ, they are powerless to make the future—any future—present. All their futures are perpetually postponed. All their promises are empty.

> Time, like life, can't be kept. It can only be given.

With my heart turned away from the present, I break my promises. I fail to love those nearest to me. I fail to love my wife, my children, my parents, my siblings. I fail to be just. In ways that should be as obvious as they are decisive, love is just a matter of time. Love is just a question of who I give my time to and, then, how I handle the giving of that gift. Time, like life, can't be kept. It can only be given. I give it by paying attention. I waste it by being distracted.

If I look forward in the wrong way, I'll ignore how fleeting the present is. I'll live as if time isn't short, as if the end isn't already at the door. I'll miss my children growing up. I'll miss my wife holding out her hand. I'll miss the chance to call my mom. I'll wake up one day, and they will be gone. I'll be out of time. I'll be alone. Once my heart starts looking forward in the wrong way, I'll go blind to the present. Even before the end comes, I will lose them. Turning away from God, my heart turns away from my family. Worshipping other gods, I won't be able to see them. I'll look right through them. They won't show up as ends in themselves. I'll just see them as means to some other, future end. Or, even more commonly, I'll just see them as an obstacle to my plans. My daughter will ask for help with an essay and I'll be too busy. My wife will ask me to fix a faucet and I'll be angry. My son will ask me to go camping and I'll make an excuse. My family, my students, my friends, my calling— it will seem like they're always getting in my way, always stealing my time, always blocking my view of where I'd rather be. I'll resent them. And once this happens, there is only one recourse. I must let my life end early. I must repent.

Repentance is the heart of Elijah's mission. His job is to "*turn* the heart of the fathers to the children, and the heart of the children to their fathers" (Malachi 4:6, emphasis added). Working only in English, it might be easy to miss that the very word translated here as "turn" is, as I've mentioned, also the Hebrew word for "repent." To repent is to turn the heart. To repent is to turn my heart back toward my children. Elijah's job is, simply, to "*repent* the hearts of the parents to their children." Then, repenting, turning my heart back to God in the present, I find both myself and my family—in all our shared weakness—already here.

20

A Welding Link

Temple work fulfills the promise God made to Abraham. Ordinances like baptism for the dead fold the past and future into the present and seal the world's families into a "whole and complete and perfect union . . . from the days of Adam even to the present time" (D&C 128:18).

Citing Malachi, Joseph Smith remarks that "it is sufficient to know, in this case, that the earth will be smitten with a curse unless there is a welding link of some kind or other between the fathers and the children, upon some subject or other" (D&C 128:18). To prevent the earth from being smitten with this curse, we need a way to weld these generations—these parents and children—together.

Here, again, time is the issue. To stop the curse, we need a new way of handling time. We need a way of welding it. But, in this case, we're not just talking about time in the abstract. Now, time has a face: when we talk about the present and the future, we're talking about parents and children. We're talking about time in the shape of a family.

To save the earth, a link must be forged. Past, present, and future generations must be welded together. Resurrections must get underway. Parents and children must be sealed. How can we fold time and seal these families? What is the welding link? "It is," Joseph says, "baptism for the dead" (D&C 128:18). Baptism is an engine for folding time. It reveals this new way of handling time. Baptism is a time machine for welding generations of families together, for turning both the past and the future back toward the present. As a type, baptism is fit for the work. We baptize by immersion "in order to answer to the likeness of the dead" because "to be immersed in the water and come forth out of the water is in the likeness of the resurrection of the dead in coming forth out of their graves" (D&C 128:12). Baptism turns death into a door. It

> Baptism is a time machine for welding generations of families together, for turning both the past and the future back toward the present.

makes death come in the middle rather than at the end. It makes death just one part of life. It practices death as a way of shuffling time and sharing lives. This is doubly true when I'm being baptized for the dead. Not only do I die, but I'm brought close to where the dead themselves are. Then both of us, if we're willing, can be resurrected together in Christ.

This is the aim of a Christian life: to die like Christ in order to share in Christ's life. When I'm crucified with Christ, I'm also resurrected with Christ. I become part of the body of Christ. The church is a type of this body—as a type, the church helps make this body present—but the church is not by itself the body of Christ. In the end, the body of Christ is the human family, "a whole and complete and perfect union, and welding together of dispensations, and keys, and powers, and glories . . . from the days of Adam even to the present time" (D&C 128:18). As the law is a type of God's original promise in Christ, the church is a type of God's eternal family.

> As the law is a type of God's original promise in Christ, the church is a type of God's eternal family.

Abraham, again, is Paul's example of how

death, resurrection, God's promise, and saved families are intertwined. God redeemed Abraham when Abraham trusted God's promise that he would "become the father of many nations" and that his seed would "be the heir of the world" (Romans 4:18, 13). But God's promise couldn't be fulfilled while Abraham was still clinging to his own life, his own expectations, and his own powers. Recall that Abraham and Sarah were much too old to have children. Their own bodies were as good as dead. If they were going to have a child, something miraculous would need to happen. As Paul puts it, Abraham, though, "being not weak in faith . . . considered not his own body now dead, when he was about an hundred years old, neither yet the deadness of Sara's womb: he staggered not at the promise of God through unbelief; but was strong in faith" (vv. 19–20). Abraham, "against hope believed in hope, that he might become the father of many nations" (v. 18).

Trusting his promise, Abraham and Sarah let themselves die in Christ. They trusted him "*who quickeneth the dead*, and calleth those things which are not as though they were," and he filled them both with new life. (Romans 4:17, emphasis added). Their bodies were, Paul says, "quickened."

As with a type, what was not yet true became as though it already was: their old bodies were full of a new shared life and, between them, a child was born.

21

The Heavens Weep

Care is a name for Christ's way of handling time. Rather than simply escaping time, Christ cares for time.

It's not easy being part of the body of Christ. Christ is vulnerable. He can be hurt. Like God, he can weep. Whatever it may mean for the Father and the Son to be all-powerful, it clearly includes the power to "shed forth their tears as the rain upon the mountains" (Moses 7:28). It includes the power to suffer, to endure loss and catastrophe and disappointment and still be God. As Christ showed Enoch—to Enoch's astonishment—"the God of heaven looked upon the residue of the people, and he wept" (v. 28). God wept because he commanded his children that "they should love one another, and that they should choose me, their Father; but behold, they are without affection, and they hate their own blood" (v. 33). God was wounded by his love for a people that had none.

Time is at the heart of this vulnerability. Time and suffering appear inseparable. Without time, nothing can change. Without change, nothing can be lost. And without loss, there would be nothing to suffer. If Christ can weep, then time must matter to him. To be vulnerable to loss, he must, in some way, be vulnerable to time. Rather than being untouched by time, it seems to me that Christ is divine because he has a particular way of handling time. He handles time with care.

> If Christ can weep, then time must matter to him. To be vulnerable to loss, he must, in some way, be vulnerable to time.

Many traditional Christian creeds deny that God can weep. They deny that God can be moved or affected or troubled by time. To protect his omnipotence, they deny that God could have a body or feel passions. But this, I think, is a brittle kind of omnipotence. It's a kind of strength that is only strong because it sidesteps all of time's troubles and life's sorrows. It's a kind of omnipotence that isn't strong enough to be vulnerable to other people and their decisions. It's a kind of omnipotence that isn't strong enough to shelter agency and bear its consequences. It's the kind of omnipotence that isn't strong enough to, as Alma puts it, suffer "pains and afflictions and temptations of every kind" (Alma 7:11).

But Christ isn't afraid of time. He isn't afraid of death. He is willing to "take upon him death, that he may loose the bands of death which bind his people." And he is willing to "take upon him their infirmities, that his bowels may be filled with mercy, according to the flesh, that he may know how to succor his people according to their infirmities" (Alma 7:12). And, more, Christ isn't even afraid to "take upon him the sins of his people, that he might blot out their transgressions according to the power of his deliverance" (v. 13).

> Christ, empowered by love, is capable of suffering. He is capable of loss. He is capable of sorrow. He can mourn.

If we confess that God *is* all powerful, then traditional ideas about his omnipotence don't go nearly far enough. They limit that power. They allow for God to have only one kind of power, the power to act. But they deny him what Enoch's vision reveals: that God also possesses the power to be acted upon.

Christ, empowered by love, is capable of suffering. He is capable of loss. He is capable of sorrow. He can mourn. The world thinks that this kind of power is just weakness, but they're wrong. "The world, because of their iniquity, shall judge him to be a thing of naught; wherefore they scourge him, and he suffereth it; and they smite him, and he suffereth it. Yea, they spit upon him, and he suffereth it, because of his loving kindness and his long-suffering towards the children of men" (1 Nephi 19:9). This power to be acted upon by life and time and choice—this power to "long-suffer"—is another name for Christ's power to care.

Let's use the word *care* (echoing the Latin word *caritas* for "charity") to name Christ's way of handling time. Let's use it to name his way of handling sickness and loss and sin and death. Care, let's say, is a name for that pure love of Christ (cf. 1 Corinthians 13:4–8). Care suffers long, is kind, envies not, and is not puffed up. It bears all things, believes all things, hopes all things, and endures all things. It makes justice possible. It never fails. Though everything else passes away, care continues. And it continues because care *is* Christ's response to the world's continual passing away.

Care, like love, names a feeling. But, more than this, care also names a kind of action. Or better, it names a certain way of doing whatever I do. I *feel* care, but I also act *with* care. Care, in this sense, doesn't name just one particular kind of action but a manner of performing any action. It's a type of Christian posture. Most any action can be done with care. The essence of care is to pay attention. Rather than being distracted by the past or the future, I pay attention in the present. I take care. I attend. I'm careful. My eyes are focused. My hands are deft and gentle. I can tie my shoes without rushing—over, under, loop, pull. I can wash a dish without fidgeting. I can stop and listen without daydreaming. I can sit in traffic without anger. Whatever I'm doing, I can do it with care. I can care. In Christ, I don't just occasionally act with care—I learn how to *live* with care.

> Though everything else passes away, care continues. And it continues because care is Christ's response to the world's continual passing away.

22

"I Give unto Men Weakness"

The weakness at the heart of life is time. But this weakness is also what leaves us open to life and responsive to God's love. This weakness is the ground that, in Christ, we share.

It's tempting to think that my present weakness makes me fundamentally different from Christ. And then, as a result, it's tempting to think that such weakness must be incompatible with Christ's divine strength. If this is true, then, to be like Christ, I would have to be untroubled by time and untouched by cares. I would have to avoid suffering rather than caring for it. But this is backwards.

Christ's strength doesn't simply rescue me from my weakness and vulnerability. As I've argued, it seems clear that his strength doesn't even save him from his own power to be acted upon. Christ is strong enough to be vulnerable. Similarly, my weakness leaves me exposed to Christ, vulnerable to his care, and open to sharing a life with him. This weakness is the ground we share. It's the ground of life. It's ground zero for God's promise. Without this weakness, I wouldn't need him. I'd be walled up, alone, inside my own perfect strength.

Christ tells Moroni that "if men come unto me I will show unto them their weakness" (Ether 21:27). And, more than that, he tells him that "I *give* unto men weakness that they may be humble; and my grace is sufficient for all men that humble themselves before me; for if they humble themselves before me, and have faith in me, then will I make weak things become strong unto them" (Ether 12:27, emphasis added). Christ has no interest in giving or preserving my petty flaws or moral failings. He aims—as I must—to fulfill the law. But Christ *does* want to both give and preserve a primal kind of vulnerability that will leave me open to life and responsive to his love. This vulnerability is essential to life. Being alive is itself a kind of weakness. To be alive is to need the world around me. To be alive is to need

> My weakness leaves me exposed to Christ, vulnerable to his care, and open to sharing a life with him. This weakness is the ground we share.

air, water, food, work, companionship. Only death has no needs. Only death has no weakness. Life's weakness is no accident, and Christ wants me to be alive. He wants me to be deeply sensitive to life—to its growing and passing, to its giving and taking—even if this hurts. Even if it hurts, he wants me to care.

This weakness at the heart of life is, simply, time. Time passes, change occurs, things are lost, people die. But this weakness is not an enemy to be destroyed. It is a gift to be cared for. It is an occasion for humility and faith. And, in light of our trust, Christ promises to meet this weakness with his strength. In this way, Christ makes "weak things become strong." Not by erasing this weakness, but by sharing it. Not by escaping time, but by folding it.

> Being alive is itself a kind of weakness. To be alive is to need the world around me.

I've spent a lot of time trying not to be weak. I've spent a lot of time trying to put myself beyond the need for care. I've worked hard. I've exercised. I've earned degrees. I've written books. I've bought new clothes. I've driven new cars. These things aren't bad in themselves. They can be good. They can, in fact, be done with care. They can be undertaken as acts of love, as means of service. But, as a rule, I haven't done this. I've treated these things more as idols than as occasions for care. I've pursued them as props for projecting a fiction of worthiness, independence, and strength. But I am tired—so tired—of pretending not to be weak. I'm tired of pretending I'm not going to die. I'm tired of pretending I don't need Christ. If I'm serious about Christ, then my only hope is to let these idols die. My only hope is to practice living with as much care and patience and attention as I can. In this sense, care is the work of no longer pretending to be strong. Care depends on finally being honest.

23

Think of Yourself as Dead

As long as we try to claim our lives as our own, we'll never be able to live them properly. As long as we try to claim our futures as our own, we'll never be properly present.

The only way to fold time is to die early. "Think of yourself as dead," Marcus Aurelius says. "You have lived your life. Now take what's left and live it properly."[1] There is something about being alive that makes it hard to live life properly. There is something about being alive that makes it hard to go slow, pay attention, be responsible, and care for life. The only way to rob death of its power is to willingly die. Christ showed

> "Think of yourself as dead," Marcus Aurelius says. "You have lived your life. Now take what's left and live it properly."

---

1. Marcus Aurelius, *Meditations*, trans. Gregory Hays (New York: Modern Library, 2003), 94.

this. The only way to save myself from the future's tyranny is to willingly sacrifice that future on God's altar. I have to give the future away. I have to let it go. I have to stop trusting in it or hoping for it. I have to hand it over to Christ. I have to consecrate the whole of it. And I have to do so *while remaining alive and embedded in time.*

In Christ, I'm dead. Whatever future remains is not mine, it's his. Whatever life is left to me is not mine, it's his. My talents? His. My money? His. My life? His. Everything he's given me? His. Even my time? Yes, please, my time. In the temple, I promise to consecrate everything to God. Part of this promise is financial. I promise, for instance, to consecrate all my money. But, in the end, the law of consecration isn't about money—it's about time. By working, I convert my time into money. Money is just time made fungible. In the end, the only thing I have to give is my time. If I cling to it, time will ruin me. If I think of my time as my own, then every unchosen obligation will feel like theft. Every call to give my time will feel like I'm being robbed of what ought to have been mine. I'll roll out of bed in the morning expecting to do as I please instead of looking to serve. Occasions for care will look like failures to succeed. Quiet moments will look like boredom. Ordinary work will look like a waste of time. The only way to be saved from this ruin is to return this time to Christ. The only way to care for time is to give it away.

Taking care is the mechanism by which we consecrate—and, thus, redeem—time. Once these things are Christ's, then I can live in him. Once I've given him my future, he can give me his present. But as long as I try to claim my life as my own, I'll never be able to live it properly. As long as I try to claim my future as my own, I'll never be properly present. I'll never be able to care for time's weakness. This is the world's oldest story: I have to die in order to live. I have to give my life away in order to find it.

> Taking care is the mechanism by which we consecrate— and, thus, redeem—time.

24

Take No Thought
for Tomorrow

Christ commands us to "take no thought
for the morrow" (Matthew 6:34). This
commandment is the key to living life
in Christ. It is the daily, practical key to
surrendering our futures, caring for
the present, and loving our families.

Folding my death into the present may or may
not help me to get ahead in life. To be fair, life
in Christ is not a useful way to live if I'm bent on
earning money, looking fabulous, being comfort-
able, winning prizes, or becoming famous. It's
not a good strategy for capturing idols. In Christ,
such things may or may not come. But, either way,
they won't matter. And, either way, I won't need
them. In Christ, I will have the one thing these
idols could never give: I'll be alive right now. And
I won't be alone.

Christ is full of impractical advice. "Take no
thought for your life," he says, "what ye shall eat,

or what ye shall drink; nor yet for your body, what ye shall put on" (Matthew 6:25). In short, "take no thought for the morrow: for the morrow shall take thought for the things of itself" (v. 34). His reason for saying this is simple: "no man can serve two masters: for either he will hate the one, and love the other; or else he will hold to the one, and despise the other." It's impossible to "serve God and mammon" (v. 24). It is impossible to serve both God and mammon because I'm not capable of doing two things at the same time. Multitasking is a myth. I can't serve two masters. Either I can die to the present for the sake of my future, or I can die to the future for the sake of the present. But I can't keep both. There's no third option.

If I choose the future, care becomes impossible. Everything and everyone will show up as a means to some other end. Care, on the other hand, looks life in the eye. It takes up everything as an end in itself, worthy of attention for its own sake. If, instead of postponing Christ, I choose to care for the present,

> Multitasking is a myth. I can't serve two masters. Either I can die to the present for the sake of my future, or I can die to the future for the sake of the present.

then I leave the future in Christ's hands. I trust him with it. Trusting Christ with the law's future fulfillment, I become capable of caring now in ways that can actually help fulfill the law. Rather than worrying about life, I live it. "Which of you by taking thought can add one cubit to his stature?" (Matthew 6:27). Not worrying, I become like "the fowls of the air: for they sow not, neither do they reap, nor gather into barns; yet your heavenly Father feedeth them. Are you not much better than they?" (v. 26). Or, I become like the lilies of the field. "Consider the lilies of the field, how they grow; they toil not, neither do they spin: and yet I say unto you, that even Solomon in all his glory was not arrayed like one of these" (vv. 28–29).

> God is the God of life, and there's only one place to find this kingdom of the living: in the present.

My job is simple: care, now. My job, right now, is "to seek ye first the kingdom of God, and his righteousness" (Matthew 6:33). God is the God of life, and there's only one place to find this kingdom of the living: in the present. Folded and welded by Christ, reordered by types and ordinances, time is already full. From the beginning, Christ has already come. As Mark says: "Jesus came into Galilee, preaching the gospel of the kingdom of God." And what was this gospel? That "the time is fulfilled, and the kingdom of God is at hand: repent ye and believe the gospel" (Mark 1:14–15). Or, as Christ tells the Pharisees: "When he was demanded of the Pharisees, when the kingdom of God should come, he answered them and said, The kingdom of God cometh not with observation: neither shall they say, Lo here! or, lo there! for, behold, the kingdom of God is within you" (Luke 17:20–21). The future is up to Christ. If I seek Christ now, then Christ can promise that these other things "will be added" when I need them (Matthew 6:33). But whether they are or aren't, that's up to him. And if trusting Christ means anything, it means trusting him with my future so that I can share his resurrected life in the present.

When I accept Christ as my master, I die early and time's polarity gets reversed. Rather than always being attracted to the future, time becomes full and the present becomes magnetic. Drawn by the pull of the present into the thick of life, I'm resurrected early. But when I'm absorbed in caring for this present world, time doesn't go away. Goals don't go away. Desires don't go away. The future doesn't go away. The law doesn't go away. They all remain in play. In the present, I care for time, I don't escape it. But now, rather than being idols, all these things become types. I still have goals, but I don't put my trust in them. These goals become types. I still have desires, but I don't put my trust in them. These desires become types. I still keep the law, but I don't put my trust in the law. I put my trust in Christ.

As a matter of course, I want things because I want something from them. I want peace. I want happiness. I want love. But only Christ can offer these things. And Christ does not offer them in the way I expect. He doesn't offer them as a *result*, he offers them as a *manner*. He doesn't offer them as a noun, he offers them as a verb (or, even better, as an adverb). That is to say, he does not give them in the way the world tries to give them. "Peace I leave with you," Christ says, "my peace I give unto you," but "not as the world giveth, give I unto you" (John 14:27).

Every day I ask the world to give me something that it can't. I ask my wife to make me feel happy. I ask my work to make me feel loved. I ask my car or my house or my clothes to give me peace. I ask a movie or a football game to make life feel exciting and meaningful. I ask the church to be what I think it ought to be. And when this doesn't work, I get bitter and go looking for something else that might have what I want. I invest some new thing with the hope that, when I get it, it could make me happy. This, though, is cruel and unfair. It's cruel because peace and happiness aren't even the *kind* of thing that the world, however willing, could give. Peace and happiness simply aren't, at bottom, a function of the world *being* a certain way. They are a function of my *relating* to the world in a certain way. They're a function of my *caring* for the world in a certain way. And when I put my trust in Christ—when I consecrate my time and treat my goals and desires as types—then I find that peace and happiness and love are already given, in plain view, in the ongoing work of caring for the world.

When I stop asking my goals and desires and loved ones to cough up what they cannot give, when I stop trying to wring some final satisfaction from them, something

> When I stop asking my goals and desires and loved ones to cough up what they cannot give, when I stop trying to wring some final satisfaction from them, something important happens.

important happens. No longer aiming through my goals, I can care for my goals. No longer aiming through my desires, I can care for my desires. No longer aiming through my loved ones, I can care for them. And no longer aiming through the law at a distant future in God's presence, I can care for the law in Christ. I can live in God's presence, now.

This is a different kind of life. In Christ, I still have goals, but, practicing care, I don't do the work for the sake of these goals. I do the work for Christ. I do the work for its own sake. I learn to love the work. I still have goals, but these goals don't own me. They don't control me. They don't master me. *I don't pin my happiness on achieving them.* Christ is my master. And then, free from the tyranny of these goals, attentive to the work, the work itself improves. I become more patient and skillful, and success becomes more likely. No longer worshipping success, I'm more likely to succeed. But even if I fail—as I consistently will—the work will have been worth doing for its own sake.

This may be especially true when it comes to God's law. I've promised to live this law. But, frequently, I will fail. I will fail in ways that are both big and small. If I worship the law rather than

Christ—if I worship the goal of succeeding in my vow to keep the law—then I'll be tempted to give up. Religion will feel like an impossible burden. I'll be angry and ashamed. But if I worship Christ rather than the law, if I love the law as Christ loves me, then I'll learn how to love the law for its own sake. *I'll learn to love the law as work worth doing for its own sake—even when I do this work imperfectly, even when I fail.*

If I stop treating the law as an idol, then I can learn to love

> If I stop treating the law as an idol, then I can learn to love the law. And when I love the law, even *trying* to fulfill the law is work worth doing.

the law. And when I love the law, even *trying* to fulfill the law is work worth doing. Success is not the work's only measure. Life won't have been wasted. My life will, in Christ, have been saved in the very act of living it.

25

Be Ye Perfect

Living and loving in Christ, this world's obvious weakness cannot stop me from seeing its present perfection. This present perfection must be taken just as seriously as its promised future perfection.

In light of Christ's care, even this present world—broken and hungry as it is—shines with a kind of perfection. This is not the glow of a future perfection, free from trouble and time, but a present one. It's not that things are no longer weak. It's not like things have suddenly become ideal versions of themselves, beyond the need for any care or correction. This world will always be vulnerable. Even at our very best, we'll always need Christ's care. Rather, in Christ, people and things can finally show up as being—perfectly—just whatever they are. No longer judging them in light of what I wanted them to be, I can actually see them. I can see their perfection. And, more, I can see what kind of care and healing they need.

This is what life boils down to. This is what it means to love someone: *their obvious weakness cannot stop me from seeing their present perfection.*

It's true that Christ asks us to "be ye therefore perfect, even as your Father which is in heaven is perfect" (Matthew 5:48). And, in the abstract, it's fair to read this verse as encouragement to aim at being better in the future. But, in context, this doesn't seem to me to be what Christ is after. In the verses that lead up to this commandment, Christ isn't urging me toward the kind of future moral perfection that might come from never breaking the law, good a goal as this may be. Instead, he's urging me in the strongest possible terms to practice, in the face of a painful and imperfect world, a certain kind of care. "Ye have heard that it hath been said, Thou shalt love thy neighbour, and hate thine enemy. But I say unto you, Love your enemies, bless them that curse you, do good to them that hate you, and pray for them

> This is what it means to love someone: their obvious weakness cannot stop me from seeing their present perfection.

which despitefully use you, and persecute you"
(Matthew 5:43–44).

If I've chosen the future over the present, then
I'll be tempted to use that future to judge the present. I'll be tempted to use that future to decide
who's worthy of my care and attention and who
isn't. Those who get in the way of that future are
my enemies. Those who can help me secure that
future are my friends. But, if I've chosen to let my
future die and, now, live in Christ, then I won't
be able to carve up the world this way. I will see
only one category: those who need care. Friend or
enemy, helpful to my future or not, everyone will
show up as needing me to bless them and care for
them.

When I do this, when I learn to handle time
with care, then I will be a child of God. "Love
your enemies," Christ says, "that ye may be the
children of your Father which is in heaven: for he
maketh his sun to rise on the evil and on the good,
and sendeth rain on the just and on the unjust"
(Matthew 5:44, 45). How does God care for the
world? What does *his* care look like? Christ is clear.
God causes his care to shine on the evil and on
the good. He sends his care like rain on the righ-
teous and the unrighteous. His care is evenhanded.

God's care is whole, not broken into parts. It's complete, not partial. This is what the Greek word for "perfection" (*teleios*) in Matthew 5:48 means: to be perfect like God is to be "whole" or "complete." But what *kind* of perfection or wholeness is at stake when Christ asks me to be perfect like my Heavenly Father is perfect? Christ appears to have just said exactly what he means: he means the kind of love that is perfect because it is *whole* and not partial. He means the kind of love that is *complete* because it cares for both those who are evil and those who are good. He means the kind of love that is whole because it cares, in whatever ways are needed, in whatever ways are appropriate, for the whole world. In Christ, life becomes simple. If something is good, I must greet it with care. If something is bad, I must greet it with care. Whatever is given, I must see it perfectly, just as it is, here and now, and greet it with care.

This is the question Christ poses to me: Can I stop mortgaging my present with a lust for the future? Can I care for my enemies like God cares for his? Can I live in Christ such that nothing can stop me from seeing—despite all of its weakness, despite all of its glaring flaws, both big and small— the world's present perfection?

This is the test. The test is simple: can I look at my son, weak and stubborn and gangly, and see his perfection? Can I look at a leaf, weak and browning and chewed on, and see its perfection? Can I watch the sun's light fail at the end of a hard day and see its perfection? Can I look at my own life—so fraught, so weak, so faltering, so inadequate, so distracted, so nearsighted—and care for it, perfectly, as Christ does? If it isn't possible to begin to see such things now, there is no coming future that could save me.

> Can I live in Christ such that nothing can stop me from seeing—despite all of its weakness, despite all of its glaring flaws, both big and small—the world's present perfection?

If anything can turn my heart back toward the present, it's this kind of care. If anything can set my resurrection in motion, it's this kind of care. If anything can break my hard heart and turn it back toward my parents and wife and children, it's Christ.

"Come, Lord Jesus" (Revelation 22:20).

Postscript

In *Moby Dick*, Ishmael barely survives his first encounter with a whale. And now, having come so close to death, his life looks different. It looks more alive. He decides, as a result, to take action and stop waiting for death. He drafts a last will and testament and asks Queequeg to be his witness. Then, Ishmael says, with his will drawn and his life sealed,

> I felt all the easier; a stone was rolled away from my heart. Besides, all the days I should now live would be as good as the days that Lazarus lived after his resurrection; a supplementary clean gain of so

many months or weeks as the case might be. I survived myself; my death and burial were locked up in my chest. I looked round me tranquilly and contentedly, like a quiet ghost with a clean conscience sitting inside the bars of a snug family vault.[1]

Ishmael preempts death and gets an early start on his next life. A stone rolls away from his heart. He sits like a quiet ghost with a clean conscience. He lives like Lazarus. He survives himself. The time that remains is, for him, a clean, supplementary gain—a grace.

Alive in Christ, I survive myself. I fold time, give back my life, and start sharing his. Baptism is my last will and testament. Buried in those waters, I deed my life to Christ. But this is just the beginning. As a daily practice in the time that remains, my work is simply to care.

This work is ordinary. And because it's ordinary, it's both easy and hard. For the most part, living in Christ, I just continue doing what I've always done. I just continue living. I eat, I sleep, I make jokes, I read, I teach, I run, I kiss. But now, in Christ, I learn to live deliberately. I learn to do

---

1. Herman Melville, *Moby Dick* (New York: Modern Library, 1992), 331.

these same things with great care. I learn to work with unbroken attention, taking one thing at a time, without hurry or fear or regret. I learn to be patient. I learn to listen. I learn to be grateful. I learn how to pray.

And having learned how to pray, I'm no longer just alive. Having learned how to pray, I live my life *as* a prayer.

Praying, I wake up in God's presence, I work in God's presence, I eat in God's presence, I lie down in God's presence. Prayer, rather than being occasional, becomes constant.

I live as Amulek advises (cf. Alma 34:17–26). I cry unto God for mercy because he is mighty to save. I cry unto him when I'm in my fields. I cry unto him when I'm in my house. I cry unto him when it's morning, when it's midday, and when it's evening. I cry unto him for my enemies. I cry unto him for my family and friends. I cry unto him for the crops of my fields and the fruit of my labors.

> And having learned how to pray, I'm no longer just alive. Having learned how to pray, I live my life *as* a prayer.

This, though, is not enough. Amulek urges me to go farther. In all this, he says, "ye must pour out your souls in your closets, and your secret places, and in your wilderness" (Alma 34:26). Instead of keeping my life for myself, I pour it out. I pour out my soul. I give it back to God—minute by minute, hour by hour, day by day—by living my life as a prayer. I pray, again and again: "not my will, but thine, be done" (Luke 22:42). Praying, I practice dying early. Praying, I practice surviving myself. Praying, I empty myself of myself.

This is possible. You don't have to spend your life watching television. You don't have to spend your life clicking on links or scrolling through feeds. You don't have to live distracted and divided and disappointed. You don't have to live a life of quiet desperation.

Pour yourself out. Live with great care.

In everyday life, this is what an early resurrection looks like. It looks like continual care. It looks like letting my heart be filled by God, "drawn out in prayer unto him continually" (Alma 34:27). It looks like learning how to "rejoice evermore" and "pray without ceasing" and "in every thing give thanks: for this is the will of God in Christ Jesus concerning you" (1 Thessalonians 5:16–18).